Garden Rules

The Snappy Synopsis for the Modern Gardener

Published by Cool Springs Press
P.O. Box 2828
Brentwood, Tennessee 37024

EAN: 978-1-59186-491-2

Library of Congress Cataloging-in-Publication Data

Jenkins, Jayme.
  Garden rules : the snappy synopsis for the modern gardener / by
Jayme Jenkins ; and Billie Brownell.
    p. cm.
  ISBN 978-1-59186-491-2 (softcover)
  1. Gardening--Popular works. I. Brownell, Billie. II. Title. III. Title:
Snappy synopsis for the modern gardener.

  SB455.J54 2011
  635--dc22

                              2010039931

First Printing 2011
Printed in the United States of America
10 9 8 7 6 5 4 3 2 1

Managing Editor: Billie Brownell, Cover to Cover Editorial Services
Developmental Editor: Jamie Chavez, WordWorks
Art Director: Marc Pewitt
Illustration: Bill Kersey, Kersey Graphics

Visit the Cool Springs Press Website at www.coolspringspress.com.
You can find this title, other Cool Springs Press books, and other
gardening books for sale at www.GardenBookstore.net.

Garden Rules

The Snappy Synopsis for the Modern Gardener

JAYME JENKINS and BILLIE BROWNELL

COOL SPRINGS PRESS

Growing Successful Gardeners™

BRENTWOOD, TENNESSEE

Acknowledgments

A special thanks to my friends and family: to my dad, for making me look up every word in the dictionary when I was a kid; to my mom, for nurturing my creative side; to Lisa, for the support and picking up my slack; to Debra Prinzing, for introducing me to the garden writing world; to Jean Ann Van Krevelen, for connecting me with Cool Springs Press.

Thanks to Roger Waynick and Cindy Games, for taking a chance on a first-time author; to Jamie Chavez, for fixing all my grammatical errors; to Bill Kersey, our illustrator; and to my patient editor and co-author Billie Brownell.

Thanks, also, to my online Facebook, Twitter, and garden community friends who tolerated all my questions and provided me with many valuable insights.

Jayme

I would like to thank the people at Cool Springs Press, all of whom have been so supportive of the *Garden Rules* concept. Specifically, a big thanks to Roger Waynick, Cindy Games, Marc Pewitt, and Jim Bashour; not only did they form the cheering squad, but they contributed ideas, as well.

I would like to thank the Cool Springs Press authors, from whom I learned so much as we worked together over the years.

I'd also like to thank my family, who are also interested in gardening and landscaping, for inspiring my garden efforts, and to my friends Jamie Chavez and Jason Owens, who listened as I shared ideas and gave their honest feedback.

And for all of you, who want a garden or landscape to be proud of, but who battle time more than anything else—I hope you find this book helps you achieve that, even a little.

Billie

Contents

Introduction

You won't often hear authors saying this, but:

THIS BOOK IS NOT FOR EVERYONE.

It really is not intended for the expert gardener, though our essential garden rules can benefit everyone (and you *can* teach old dogs new tricks). Gardening is a wonderful pastime, but like many hobbies, you have to devote *time* to it—time you think you may not have. (Heck, even the word *pastime* talks about *time*.)

Rather, this book is for those of us—like *you*—who enjoy gardening, who may be newlyweds, apartment dwellers, or new homeowners; those who are interested in having an attractive home landscape but who may not have much garden "know-how"; and those who want to learn a little more. It's for those of us who face all kinds of competition for our time.

Competition? Oh yeah, you know—it's also called "Life." Our careers, families, social lives, and other interests are just a few *things* that demand our attention. Where is gardening supposed to fit in? You may have wandered into the gardening world through the slow-food movement, the growing concern about food safety, or decided some pretty flowers would soften the look of your balcony railing. Whatever the reason, your interest has been piqued and you're wondering what your next step should be. Look no further! *Garden Rules* is for you.

As authors, we don't claim to offer the only advice in town, but we do claim to have the snappiest, CliffsNotes® version of abbreviated, cut-to-the-chase advice for incorporating gardening into your life—not the other way around. Nor do we claim to offer every garden rule—it's a small book— but we cover all the "biggies."

Some of the biggies are soil, sun, watering, fertilizing, and all that other stuff, as well as planting, pests, garden design, and time management. We believe that our garden rules, written in ways that you can easily remember, will help you garden more successfully. What does *successfully* mean? Well, that's up to you. It might mean you feel a little more garden-smart, or are less overwhelmed, or manage time in the garden better, or you learn more about gardening within your environment, or you have just a little knowledge edge over your friends.

I, Jayme, am a pushover for DIY projects. I love taking an idea (or even copying someone else's) and making it into reality. I was the kid who begged my parents for the latest Play-Doh® and LEGO® sets, then cheered, "Hey, Mom, look what I did!"

Gardening feeds my desire to imagine, create, and enjoy the rewards of a job well done. I'd be lying if I said I don't silently gloat every time my friends and neighbors compliment me on my garden.

I've heard almost every excuse in the book for not starting a garden. But, there *is* a garden for every person, every budget, and every lifestyle. If you're limited by time, start small; if you're on a budget, learn to start from seed (and *grow* patience, too— sorry, I couldn't resist); if creativity is not your strong suit, buy a premade design; if you have no yard, grow a windowsill or balcony garden; if you lack the know-how, keep reading this book.

I, Billie, am so happy to have this opportunity to share with you those lessons I learned the best (sometimes the hard way) that may give you a few shortcuts and ideas. Even though I *love* being outside, I've found that gardening is just one of many outdoor activities I enjoy, which include riding horses and hiking. But when it comes to a choice between riding my horse or gardening, well, truthfully, there isn't a contest. *Giddy up!*

As authors, we encourage you to give gardening a try—you may find you love it. But even if you don't ever become an avid gardener, we hope this book will help you find a happy balance between it and your life . . . and that you find the time to do it *well enough*.

Jayme and Billie

Rule Number One: There Are No Rules

I LIVE IN A NEIGHBORHOOD that feels completely safe today, but the remnants of a time when it was "not so safe" remain in the form of reinforced doors and backyard security lights. The light from the security lamp of the house next door is so bright I can literally read by it, which I often do during the summer once the sun goes down and temperatures moderate. (Actually, the light is so bright I can read by it *inside* my home.)

One time, when I was again running late, getting home at 8:00 p.m., I realized that I could do a tremendous amount of gardening by this light. I began to use the time that I had—albeit nontraditional—to water potted plants, to tidy up, and to deadhead blooms because that was the best time I had. It isn't what the other neighbors do (at least, I don't think so) but it works for me.

Garden Rules' Number One rule is that you can write your own rules—if you find something that works for you, then there's nothing that says you have to do it the "traditional" way. (BB)

If You Can Only Do One Thing, Keep the Lawn Mowed

WHEN I BOUGHT MY FIRST HOUSE, aka my first yard, a family member said, "Just keep the yard looking nice and the neighbors will love you." Given that it appeared as though the neighbors were trimming their grass with nail clippers, this seemed more than a little bit overwhelming.

What I discovered was that keeping the lawn mowed was really the main requirement. No one wants to live next to "that kind" of neighbor who doesn't keep up with Joneses in the lawn-mowing department. It makes everything look sloppy. And I found that *I* liked it better when the lawn was nicely mowed because it created a welcoming feel; I *liked* pulling into the driveway.

There is a powerful psychological effect of making something nice and neat the last thing you see when you leave and the first thing you see upon your return home. That's why de-cluttering your house is considered critical to a sense of well-being.

And lest you think this rule is in conflict with "Rule Number One: There Are No Rules," bear in mind that peer pressure is one of the most powerful influences on the planet. (BB)

Be Kind to Our Planet. It's the Only One We've Got.

TRUTHFULLY, enough said.

But because we're (almost) paid by the word, like Dickens, let me emphasize that the natural world works in astonishing ways and *everything* is connected. It's the most marvelous set of relationships you can imagine.

If you choose to use a chemical (and I've got a gallon of glyphosate in my garage right now), be mindful that it does not just kill weeds or pest insects. It can kill *everything*. Glyphosate is effectively a soil sterilizer. That means it kills not just weeds, but earthworms, fungi, beneficial bacteria, beneficial insects—just about everything it comes into contact with. It can drift and run off your lawn, down the street, into the storm drain, and down to the watershed, where its effects can persist for quite some time.

There are some far-reaching consequences to using chemicals. Read the directions, follow the directions, be mindful. (BB)

A Watched Garden
Never Grows

PATIENCE IS A VIRTUE but we've been conditioned to expect instantaneous *everything*. Cell phones allow us to send and receive messages instantly, social media such as Twitter let us know where Paris Hilton is at any moment, and television commercials have trained our brains to anticipate a new stimulus *every 30 seconds*. It is no wonder our attention spans have shortened and our desire for instant gratification has heightened. We expect everything to happen at 3G speed.

Think about the commercials you've seen for gardening products that promise flowers twice as big as usual and mountains of tomatoes. Fast-talking spokesmen tell us we can have the garden of our dreams in no time—practically overnight! The truth is, if it sounds too good to be true, it probably is.

The key to enjoying your time in the garden is to keep your expectations realistic. Seedlings take days to sprout. Flower buds take time to develop. Perennials like hostas, peonies, bleeding hearts, and Siberian iris take a couple seasons to reach maturity. Trees will take years to provide shade.

Nature does not operate at twenty-first–century speed, and Nature *always* wins. (JJ)

Plants Can't Read

EVEN THOUGH THE WORTH of a garden often exceeds its cost, there is an understandable tendency to treat gardening or any kind of landscaping very seriously. Gardening is *not* always particularly inexpensive. There are plants, and fertilizers, and mulch—it can all add up.

But one of the greatest advantages on our side is that plants can't read. They don't know if they are "supposed" to die. That's why it can be fun to try new plants that you really want to try (usually perennials or shrubs due to inherent cost, but also trees if you are a gambler). I have a 'Black & Blue' salvia that is on the knife edge of my hardiness zone. But it has wintered over and it's *spectactular*. It is so worth growing—even as an annual—that I'll definitely replant if it falls victim to winter.

Don't be afraid to experiment. The worst that can happen is a plant might die. The best that could happen is that it will live and prosper.

So lighten up; they're just plants. Nobody dies; nobody gets hurt. They're just plants. (BB)

Plant the Right Plant in the Right Place

PLANTING THE RIGHT PLANT in the right place is such a classic garden rule that entire books have been written with that phrase as the title. Plants have needs, just like we do. Some like it hot, cool, wet, dry, sunny, shady—and all variations in between. Heck, some even like it humid! If I had known this rule when I first started gardening, I would have spent quite a bit less money replacing plants.

There are five things to think about: hardiness zone, soil, sun, water, and pests.

With the exception of annuals and almost all vegetables (which are nearly all annuals), knowing your hardiness zone is important. This refers to the coldest it might get in the winter (on average). Therefore, if you want to grow a lilac, which needs winter chill, it won't happen if you live in Florida.

With soil, you pretty much have to play the hand you're dealt. It's virtually impossible to change soil pH (which means how acidic or alkaline it is) without major effort. But I recommend amending your soil and mulching. You'll probably have some combination of clay or sandy soil. If the plant tag recommends well-drained soil and you have mostly clay (which doesn't drain well), you'll have to do *something* so it will drain better. Mixing the soil with composted leaves or some other organic amendment (even mulch) will help.

If the plant tag says full sun, believe it. It's easy to assume that you know how much sun your yard gets, but it changes during the day. I once took photographs—of what I thought was a sunny spot—every hour during the day, and was shocked at how much shade it really got. Make sure you really know how much sun a spot is getting. Sure, you can certainly water a thirsty plant more, but do you really want to drag a hose or watering cans around? You will always be fighting nature when you have a plant that needs extra water because it's getting too much sun, or it is just naturally thirsty to begin with.

Critters can be more than garden pests and diseases, though there are plenty of those. I'm talking about deer, and rabbits, and moles. There are entire books devoted to deer-proofing your garden, which ought to tell you something. But there are things they don't like to eat. Find them.

It all comes down to this: Match your plants to the growing conditions in your garden—not the other way around. (BB)

Make Friends
With an Expert

ALTHOUGH I would never discount the value of a good book, there is nothing like firsthand advice from an experienced gardener.

That might be a family member or a neighbor with a beautiful yard. Your local nursery or garden center has some of the best advice you'll find; even some of the big-box stores can have really knowledgeable staff (although that's hit or miss). Experienced gardeners can help advise you about local soil needs, give you tips on tools, and show you which types of flowers grow well together. Whoever your local expert may be, make sure to ask lots of questions. Don't be shy—most gardeners love to talk about their gardens!

Don't automatically turn to the Internet as an authority, because there is a lot of misinformation floating around out there. Trusted sources are well-known garden authors, universities, reputable organizations, and local extension services. Think .edu rather than .com. Be wary of garden forums, as some folks who are not necessarily experienced may fake it well. You can always consider someone's word as a helpful tip to point you in the right direction, just not gospel truth. (JJ)

It's a Poor Workman Who Blames His Tools

THAT'S A GREAT LITTLE SAYING, but the truth is that having decent garden tools, and the right ones, will make gardening fall more into the fun category.

Anyone who is just starting gardening needs a few basic tools including:

a **shovel** — the pointy-end kind, plus a garden spade that is more rectangular on the end is *great*

a **trowel** — indispensible

a **pair of garden gloves** — get the best kind you can afford

a **weeder** — very handy although I literally once used a flat-head screwdriver and it did just fine

a **leaf rake** — not just for raking leaves but also for raking beds and smoothing mulch

a **wheelbarrow** — very helpful if you have the room to store one

a **watering can** — at least one but I have three

a **garden hose** — the best you can afford

Once you have these to start, you can add more to your collection as you become a better gardener. (BB)

Plant Seedlings
Before Seeds

I HAVE A FRIEND who purchased several hundred yards of beautiful (and pricey) yarn made of Icelandic wool—before she even learned to knit.

I once purchased a table saw to build a wine cabinet for my kitchen. Why start with a cutting board or step stool when you can start a first-time project with a wine rack? Right!

I hesitate to squelch anyone's excitement about starting a garden from seed, but if you are a casual or part-time gardener, start with store-bought nursery seedlings until you get a little experience. There are definitely some skills to be learned before sowing a garden from seed—but in the meantime you can have a delightful display of fountain grasses, lantanas, pink wave petunias, or whatever strikes your fancy, for very little effort by buying transplants. (Google "annual flowerbed combinations" for more sun or shade design ideas.) (JJ)

What's Done Can *Usually* Be Undone

WHEN I first began gardening, I was so overwhelmed by the idea of planting in a new bed, my mind would buzz with questions: Where should *this* plant go? What should the *next* plant be? How *far away* should I plant them?

I realize now that this anxiety is really unnecessary. If you find yourself worrying about these things, a simple design plan can take the edge off and eliminate the need to answer those burning questions when you're up to your elbows in dirt. And one of the really awesome things about a garden is, unlike a fancy stamped concrete patio, a plant can usually be easily moved if you don't like your original design. Virtually nothing is set in stone (literally).

Note that summertime is not a good time to relocate plants to different areas of the garden. Underneath the beating sun, plants experience tremendous stress and are unlikely to acclimate to their new homes very well. The best time to transplant is when temperatures are cooler and rain is plentiful; depending on where you live, that's probably fall but it could be winter. (JJ)

Forget About Hardiness if You Plant Only Annuals

I FEEL A BIT INTIMIDATED by the USDA Hardiness Zone map, probably because I am map-challenged.

The map is a graphic representation of the United States split into eleven hardiness zones indicating the *average* low temperatures expected in winter. (Hardiness zones do not take summer high temperatures into consideration.) For example, I live in Zone 6b, and—on average—we can expect winter temperature will drop no colder than about zero to minus 5 degrees. Usually, it won't be colder than that (although it *could* be . . .).

Knowing your zone is important if you are planting lots of perennials, including trees, shrubs, and perennial flowers. But it's irrelevant if you plant only annuals (including virtually all vegetables) because an *annual* isn't affected by wintertime cold temperatures.

Perhaps more important (though flawed) is the AHS Heat Zone. There is a world of difference in the plants that can be grown in the Shetland Islands versus south Alabama, although they share a similar hardiness zone. Learn both if you are planting perennials, but don't bother if you're not. (BB)

Baby Transplants Like They Were Babies

TRANSPLANTS ARE EVERYTHING that comes already growing in pots or containers: annuals, perennials, trees, shrubs, roses, vegetables. Other than seeds, virtually everything else we plant is a transplant. And you should think of transplants as if they were newborns. It's a shock to their systems to be moved from their "home" and shoved into the ground in spring or early summer, often during the hottest part of the day (because that's when you got home with them from the nursery, all fired up and excited).

It's much better to give transplants a little time to adjust by setting them in the shade for a day or so and then planting at dusk or early evening, or on a cloudy day. Don't leave them on your driveway or patio because the reflected heat and light from that surface is enormous. The main reason that "fall is for planting" has become such a big thing is because heat stress is so much less, so a plant can adjust to its new surroundings.

Water is really important; if the roots dry out before you can plant, then that's it—they won't regrow. So keep the transplants moist (but not wet) and water after you plant. You can set smaller transplants (in their containers) inside a larger tray partly filled with water. They'll suck up moisture as they need it from the drainage holes in the containers.

There are special transplant fertilizers that can be added to the water but you don't want to fertilize too much. Fertilizing encourages growth and a transplant needs to focus on adapting to its new home first.

When you're getting new plants out of their containers (or unwrapping the burlap of a larger balled-and-burlapped shrub or tree), be gentle, so you handle stems and roots as little as possible. This is harder than it sounds for larger shrubs or trees; it's very tempting to grab them by the trunk and manhandle them.

If new plants are struggling, think about moving them back into shade (if they're in a container). If they're already in the ground, there are shade cloths but they're mainly for commercial growers. You can fake something similar for smaller plants, though, using cardboard propped up so the plant is protected from afternoon sun. If it's an annual or perennial that came loaded with buds, take a deep breath and pinch off most of them. It will all be okay. (BB)

If the Tag Says "Creeping"—Believe It!

DO YOU EVER READ REALTOR ADS? I love them, and especially love to decipher the code words, such as *dollhouse*. What the realtor really means is that the house is so tiny only a doll could fit in it. There's far more real truth in advertising in the garden world, but you have to know the code.

One year, I bought a *tiny* lemon balm at the flea market. As the seller handed it to me, she commented, "If they like their spot, they'll spread." Boy, did it ever. By the time I dug it out, it had taken over a section of my yard, kept inbounds only because it was a terraced backyard, and the lemon balm was restrained to one terrace.

In the plant world, red-flag code words for "aggressive" include: *fast-spreading*, *prolific*, *creeping*, *robust*, *naturalizing*, and *rampant grower*. They all mean the same thing: if left to its own devices, the plant will get out of hand, and quickly! Mints, English ivy, lily-of-the-valley, ajuga, and violets are all in this group. You can avoid them altogether, or plant them in containers to keep them under control, because they *will* spread. (BB)

Hold a Dress Rehearsal Before Planting

I AM PROUD TO SAY it only took a few times of planting and then digging things back up before I realized I should position annual and perennial transplants in their beds by first placing the containers on the ground. Then I could more easily see if a plant worked with the other plants already there, and if I had enough (or too many). I've dug up taller plants that I'd put in front before I realized they would hide the plants farther back in the bed. It's also easier to "see" color combinations if they are in bloom already.

This is a good time to remember that plants grow and—God willing—won't always be the size they are when you bought them as transplants. Check the plant tags again to make sure you know about how tall they'll grow.

You can do the same thing with shrubs and trees. I usually use my wheelbarrow to move them around if possible. (This is much harder to do with larger trees; you'd better have a pretty good idea where they are going to go if a truck has to deliver them.) (BB)

Misery Loves Company

DO YOU REMEMBER that kid in grade school you felt sorry for because the classroom bully picked on him? Day after day, the bully relentlessly focused on the one kid he perceived as the weakest, and proceeded to pick away at him without mercy.

Well, bullies and plant disease have one thing in common: finding a weakness.

In the same way that bullies only pick on the kids they think are too weak to retaliate, pests and diseases will prey on already weakened plants.

No plant is really ever immune from nature's bullies, but healthy plants can withstand the daily attacks. The first step is to bring home good-looking, healthy, strong plants from your local nursery. Resist the urge to feed an unhealthy plant with an overdose of fertilizer. This is a prime example of too much of a good thing—it simply won't help. (JJ)

You Get What You Pay For
. . . Most of the Time

LIKE all rules, there are exceptions, but you can often evaluate a plant's quality based on price because you get what you pay for with "bargain" plants. Keep in mind the appearance of a plant is everything. Plants will visibly let you know when they are unhealthy. If the leaves are yellowing or droopy, these are signs of stress that could lead to health problems down the road. If the edges of the leaves are brown, the plant may have had inconsistent watering. But if everything looks lovely, then specifically consider the cost. When the bargain shopper in you ventures to a big-box garden store and finds a "too good to be true" sort of deal on a plant in the middle of July, it probably *is* too good to be true. Many times a store is simply looking to get rid of spring overstock, and their problem becomes your problem.

I have yet to see a 50 percent off plant sale that offers sturdy stock of lush green leaves holding flowers that are just waiting to burst into bloom. You probably won't find this, either. (JJ)

"Perennial" Does Not Mean the Same Thing as "Living Forever"

WHEN I FIRST BECAME INTERESTED in gardening, I hired a landscaper to install a perennial bed. Wow, I thought, that was a good investment! Imagine my surprise when, the next year, several of the "perennials" failed to appear because they didn't survive the winter. This was my first introduction to the fact that "perennial" simply is not the same thing as "living forever."

Every plant, even trees, has a natural lifespan. They don't live forever (although the bristle-cone pine is making a pretty good run). The definition of a perennial is a plant that lives more than *two* seasons. Some plants, such as trees, may live many, many years, while others, such as the perennial flowers in my first bed, bought the farm pretty quickly.

This is why it's important, particularly with trees and shrubs (which are harder to plant and very hard to move later), to know which of them have a generally shorter lifespan overall than other types you can choose to plant.

You can even the playing field by using good cultural practices, but count your blessings when your perennial flowers return more than a few seasons. (BB)

Herbs Are
"Black Thumb" Proof

IF YOU THINK you have a "black thumb," then herbs are perfect for you. They are practically foolproof. Some, such as mint, will grow in nearly any type of soil, in sun or shade, can survive in extreme heat or under inches of snow, and barely need *any* maintenance (mint is also aggressive, and might be better grown in a pot). Some are great self-sowers, like oregano, chamomile, and borage. The key to growing most herbs is excellent drainage, sun, and—shockingly—basically infertile soils.

You can eat herbs fresh nearly year-round; just pick them in the morning when their aromatic oils are the strongest. And they dry like a dream! To create your own fully stocked spice rack, bundle cut herbs together, place them in a paper bag, and hang them to dry in a warm, airy room. This works well with herbs such as bay leaves, dill, marjoram, oregano, rosemary, summer savory, and thyme. For herbs with higher moisture content, such as basil, chives, mint, and tarragon, just pop them in your freezer to have them ready to use year-round. You can even freeze herbs in ice-cube trays with a little water. (JJ)

Plants Never Have To Go on Diets

UNLIKE PEOPLE, plants *never* have to go on diets (darn them!), nor should they. With very few exceptions—heirloom vegetables and herbs being examples—more nutrition for plants means bigger, better, stronger.

Especially in the case of potted annual and perennial plants, whose containers don't have the capacity to "store" nutrients, it's important to feed plants every time you water them, or to mix long-lasting fertilizer into the potting medium. Trees and shrubs need food, too, just not as often.

The "Big Three" nutrients include nitrogen, phosphorus, and potassium (abbreviated by their chemical names to NPK). These are the basic building blocks for plant life; without them, most plants cannot live. Most commercial fertilizer formulas are based solely on NPK. Secondary nutrients include sulfur, calcium, and magnesium. There are a few other micronutrients, and it doesn't hurt to know a little bit about them to know if you need a specialty fertilizer.

You can tell if a plant is starving if it has yellow or pale leaves (unless it's a type with that as a natural color variation) or if it's puny (few flowers, smaller leaves). Don't wait—dish up! (BB)

An Ounce of Prevention Is Worth a Gallon of Roundup®

INVARIABLY IN SPRING, as I am thinking about creating a new annual or perennial bed, I will wish that I had planned things just a *bit* sooner.

That is, I'll be looking at turf that must be dug out fairly quickly to avoid planting the beds too late in the season. By the time my linear thinking has reached this point, I nearly always use Roundup to kill the grass in order to prepare the bed.

Don't get me wrong—I use chemicals, but I try to use them judiciously. But preparing a bed is one case where a little planning could have gone a long way. I could design the size and shape of the bed and spread newspaper or landscape fabric (held down by bags of mulch) to kill the grass over the winter. By the time spring rolls around, it would be a much easier job to dig out dead grass.

Getting a handle on the weeds growing in the cracks and crevices of a driveway or sidewalk by digging them out when they are *small*, before they develop those strong roots, is another example.

Just a little bit of prevention and planning will go a long way. (BB)

Read the Label.
Read the Label.
Read the Label.

IT'S AN INDIVIDUAL CHOICE to use pesticides (and I do), but have you ever pulled out the label on a container? It unfolds and unfolds— and it's in micro-type almost impossible to read. By their very nature, pesticides are designed to *kill*, well, pests, and often pose some threat to humans, animals, and the environment.

If you read it, and you should, you'll find there are many cautions that tell you how to safely handle the chemicals. The label will have the common and brand names, the chemical name, the active ingredients, the target pest(s), directions for use, first aid, how to dispose of the container properly, and other information. All of these are important, but pay particular attention to the target pest, to make sure the pesticide is actually effective against the one you're trying to control. It's pointless to use a pesticide against mites (you'd have to use a miticide against mites); and you will needlessly expose yourself and the environment.

In order of increasing risk, the words "Caution," "Harmful," and "Danger" appear on the label. Remember: using a pesticide contrary to the label is possibly ineffective and it's against the law. (BB)

If You Want Visitors, Put Out the Buffet

ONE OF THE BIG ATTRACTIONS of gardening is that we *want* butterflies and bees (and hummingbirds and all kinds of other beneficial creatures) to visit. Butterflies are beautiful, bees are fascinating—and kids *love* them. Planting for beneficial "critters" is a great way to get children interested in gardening.

But they need our help. It's estimated that butterfly populations have declined 40 percent in the last thirty years, and honeybees are also under stress. Bees pollinate *one-third* of all the foods we eat. What would we do without them? Well, we'd be a lot thinner.

There are all kinds of garden store signs that identify nectar-producing flowers for butterflies— pentas, butterfly bush, salvias, zinnia, coneflowers, phlox, and butterfly weed are a few—but I have *never* seen a sign telling us that in order to have butterflies, we need to plant for all their life stages. That means they have to have a place to drink (a pan of damp sand is fine), a place to find shelter, a place to lay eggs, and food for the caterpillars (their larvae).

Caterpillar host plants vary by the type of butterfly, but some common ones are parsley, dill, fennel, rue, Queen Anne's lace, hollyhocks, snapdragons, rose of Sharon, lupines, milkweed (the *only* plant that monarch caterpillars will eat), and lots more. I hope it goes without saying that butterflies and caterpillars are insects, and pesticides will kill them.

Bees like pretty much the same things. They need water; they like many of the same flowers as butterflies, especially native plants. Some of bees' favorite plants are coreopsis, catmint, salvias, cosmos, gaillardia, lavender, scented geraniums, lamb's ears, sunflowers, and lots more. It's easy to look on the Internet to see the plants they most like for your area. Then, plant the flowers in bigger clusters so they can see them and hop from flower to flower. If you must spray a pesticide, do it after dusk when bees are not moving around. They're most active from spring until late fall, when they go "dormant" (they don't actually hibernate, but they hang out in their hive and get *really* slow).

I once saw *twenty* swallowtail caterpillars devouring my parsley. It was such a huge thrill that I didn't care that they ate it all. But it's very sad to me that it's been years since I've seen many honeybees.

Imagine your world without either of them. Now do something about it. (BB)

Organic Doesn't Equal Safe

THE MOVEMENT toward organic pest control is a good thing. But there is a great temptation to equate organic with safe and that's not always the case. In fact, there are some genuinely toxic substances that are completely organic.

Rotenone, which is completely derived from plant sources, is a pesticide, miticide, and it kills fish (fishicide? …). There have been some studies linking rotenone to Parkinson's disease, which has led to a re-examination of its safety. It's a similar story for pyrethrins, the base for many organic products. Plus, there is no guarantee that an organic is inherently better at doing its job than a synthetic.

The safer organic products to use include insecticidal soaps, Bt (*Bacillus thuringiensis*, a naturally occurring bacterium), and kaolin clay (used as a dust to annoy some insects). There are also naturally disease-resistant plants, barriers such as floating row covers (mainly used for veggie gardening), and using compost and fish emulsion as fertilizers.

Just read the label and decide if it's something you don't mind in your garden, on your skin, in your lungs. If you do mind, then find something else. (BB)

Denial (of the Environment) Is Not Just a River in Egypt

ZONE OR ENVIRONMENT DENIAL is a touchy subject that refers to the practice of growing plants outside their hardiness zone (the area where they are naturally equipped to deal with the weather in terms of average cold temperatures) or other conditions like heat, wind, and drought. Some gardeners argue that you should grow whatever you darn well please in your own garden, since it is your own time and money at stake. Others argue that there are environmental consequences for nursing plants that are not native to your local environment.

Consider lawns. When I lived in Arizona, I was shocked at the number of homeowners who had thick, green lawns in the middle of the desert. Even if you *have* an extra $1,000 a month to spend on your water bill, doesn't this seem a bit irresponsible? Water, especially treated water, is too valuable to waste.

I'm not here to take sides. But you really should care about the local resources a plant will consume, and your time and money. The plant kingdom is vast; even if you only shop within your zone, you will have lots of plants from which to choose. (JJ)

The Bigger the Leaf, the Harder It Drinks

IF YOU LOOK at rosemary you can see that it has leaves shaped more like needles than standard leaves. That's because rosemary evolved in a drier climate (the Mediterranean) and having smaller leaves is a water-conserving feature. The smaller the leaf area, the less a plant transpires (which is similar to evaporation) by moving water from its tissues to the surrounding air.

Other signs that plants have adapted to using little water are hairy leaves and fleshy leaves. Cacti have spines instead of leaves, and fleshy pads that shrink when water availability is low and expand when there is rain.

This is a good thing to know, especially if you live in a dry climate or where there are water restrictions (and water restrictions are coming for everyone—soon). It doesn't mean you cannot plant what you want but it *does* mean you'll know what to expect: broad-leafed plants may be thirsty *all the time*.

Signs of thirsty plants are: leaves curling up, footprints left in grass will stay visible instead of disappearing, leaves wilting, and leaves dropping off as the plant (often a tree) tries to save itself. (BB)

Bugs: The Good, the Bad, and the Ugly

BUGS—your garden can't live without 'em. Personally, sometimes I wish mine could, but if you grow it, they will come. There are ways designed to rid your garden of "bad" bugs, but there are "good" bugs too. So how do you tell the difference? And if you get rid of the bad bugs, what will the good ones eat? What will the frogs, salamanders, and birds eat?

As annoying as bugs may be, they definitely serve a purpose. Okay, maybe not on your bathroom ceiling, but they do have an important role in your garden. (Then again, the spiders in your home wouldn't be there without other bugs for them to eat.)

Yes, you need to watch your roses for aphids that will suck the life out of them, and your cabbages for caterpillars that will munch on the leaves. But don't assume all bugs are bad. Good bugs are called "beneficials" and include praying mantis, ladybugs, parasitic wasps (which actually feed on real pests), and spiders. Learn the difference before you declare warfare, chemical or otherwise. (JJ)

Never Allow a Vine to Grow Beyond the Reach of Your Ladder

BINDWEED, a vine (and also a weed), grows so much, so fast, it can strangle a plant (and you, if you move slowly) seemingly overnight. It's very Stephen King.

Vines are great plants and can solve many landscape problems, such as providing summertime shade or adding privacy. But many are rampant growers and can take over if you don't get the upper hand, and I mean *fast*. Some ornamental vines, like porcelain vine, are so aggressive they have been placed on invasive plant lists; you should check the list for your state.

Some vines that need a lot of pruning are wisteria, honeysuckles, and morning glory. Wisteria is also so heavy that it needs sturdy supports to hold the weight of it. You should never allow these vines to grow beyond the reach of your ladder.

There are civilized vines that behave themselves. Some of these are clematis and jasmine; another is Carolina jessamine, which has beautiful yellow flowers. Mandevilla is a tropical vine that's great.

There's no need to be afraid of vines but be ready to move quickly if you spot one behind you. (BB)

You Won't Panic If You Go Organic

RECENTLY, I was looking for an ant repellent. Every product I picked up noted extreme cautions against using the product if one had children, pets, or if you wanted to live to see another day.

If you are a vegetable gardener—and even if you're not, I'll bet you are an eater—the organic debate is a critical one on which to take a stand. There are many pros and cons, from organic edibles having a higher nutritional level balanced against the need to feed a hungry world.

Although I've stated in other garden rules that using pesticides is a personal choice—and it is—I've decided that, for thin-skinned edibles, organic products (safe ones) are the way to go. It's difficult to see pesticide contamination, but it's safe to assume that you cannot wash it all off. So for anything that has a thin skin between it and a pesticide—strawberries, apples, tomatoes, potatoes, peaches, greens, and so forth—I'm voting for being as safe as possible. For edibles that have a thicker skin or a rind that can be peeled—melons, corn, onions, sweet potatoes, cabbage—I think it's safe enough to be more flexible. (BB)

The Allergist's Garden

UNTIL I moved to Nashville, I had no idea how miserable allergies can make you. But after living in "Allergy Central" I now dread spring, especially when juniper pollen is drifting about. And I'm not the only one; it's estimated thirty-five million Americans suffer from seasonal allergies (not to mention asthma).

What I didn't know until recently is that many landscape plants are male, because the seeds or fruit, aka "litter," produced by the female plants are not desirable—sweetgum for example. But it's the male plant that produces pollen. Because plant breeders have learned to propagate plants by cloning only male plants, virtually all of those sold are males.

What can you do to create an allergy-free garden? Well, you can plant more female plants, which will "trap" pollen (oh, those old stereotypes never go away), use gravel instead of mulch for paths, don't let weeds go to seed, keep the lawn mowed (especially if it's Bermuda), and plant shrubs and flowers that naturally produce less pollen (forsythia, hydrangea, tulip, and azalea, for example). Go online to check out plant options that are best for your area. And Live Free and Breathe Easy! (BB)

Plant Murder Is
Not a Felony

SOMEWHERE along the garden path, I got this idea that I could not, *ever*, eliminate a plant that was installed in the landscape, especially if it were a tree or shrub. For years I put up with an overgrown, aggressive holly that was one of the foundation plantings to my home. I spent hours pruning it back to prevent it from absorbing the house.

I hated it.

Finally, I'd had enough. I cut it down, dug out the roots, and instantly became a happier person. It was freeing. (I wish I could say I also lost weight, but that just didn't happen.)

It's *okay* to get rid of anything you do not like. Plant murder is not a felony in this country (though I've heard it may be in England). It does not matter if it's young, old, dying, in the way, a garden thug, or just plain ugly—if a plant is not working for you, then move it, rip it out, or give it away. Obviously, if you have something that has intrinsic value—perhaps it's a historic tree—then you should reconsider this advice. But that situation affects few of us. (BB)

Train Your Grass by Watering Less Often, But Longer

I OFTEN SEE people holding a hose to water their garden beds, shrubs, and lawn. But most people will *never* stand still long enough to really water the garden as it needs to be watered, and that not only wastes water, it trains plants—especially grass—to be lazy.

Turfgrass roots grow to the depth they must to find water. If they find water near the surface, that's exactly how much they'll work. (Does this sound like kids to anyone other than me?) If they have to dig down deep to find water, then the grass will be healthier in the long run and will be able to sustain itself during periods of minor drought.

It's much better to water fewer times, but of longer duration, so roots learn to grow down farther. This also means grass roots will try harder than weed roots, which typically are closer to the surface. When the going gets tough, tough grass will survive but weeds won't. For those living in areas of water restrictions, watering duration is often regulated. It may be that you'll have to switch to a grass that can live on less water (or—gasp!—give up the lawn completely). (BB)

When the Sun Is Done, Put Up the Hose

THIS WAS A REALLY HARD LESSON to learn, particularly because I often have more time in the evenings than in the mornings. But it really *is* better for plants—with the possible exception of container plants—to water them as the temperature (that is, the sun) is rising, not setting.

The reason for this is wet leaves can lead to fungal diseases, particularly in a climate like the one I live in, where summer humidity is like a wet towel. The ground and leaves can stay damp a long, long time.

What I do is wind a soaker hose through my beds, and turn on the faucet (by hand) when the beds need to be watered. I'll let it run as I'm getting ready for work and then turn it off after an hour or so. This waters only the ground—not the leaves— and you control that it's within the drip zone.

While we're on the subject of watering, it's worth the money to get a good hose. There is a huge difference between the good ones and the cheap ones. Don't hesitate; get the good kind. It will become your new best friend. (BB)

Plants Get Stressed Out Too

PLANTS get stressed, too, from all kinds of reasons, such as too little water, too much water, too hot, too cold, too much fertilizer, the wrong kind of fertilizer . . . it's beginning to stress me out to think about it.

The tricky part is the signs can be the same for different causes. Leaves will wilt if a plant is getting too little water and if it's getting too much. Dig down a few inches; if it's dry, it's probably too little water. If it's damp, then too much water is forcing oxygen out of the soil. Wilting can also be from heat stress. If the plant looks better in the evening or when it's cooler, it's probably due to heat. (Trees will often shed leaves as a reaction to heat stress. Tomatoes, peppers, and beans will often "abort" their flowers if it's too hot.) Off-color leaves (yellow or pale green) can be a sign of too little fertilizer or not enough of the right kind (usually nitrogen).

It's confusing, and lots of other gardeners are baffled too. So don't waste time, especially if it's something of landscape value. Ask an expert! (BB)

Sometimes It *Is* Too Wet

IT SOUNDS LIKE such a convenient excuse for getting out of yard work: it's too wet to do anything. But the truth is that sometimes it *is* too wet to work in the ground (with the possible exception of container plants, which grow in a potting medium instead of dirt).

Soil compacts *very* easily and once it has done so, it can take years to rebound, if it ever does. That's why wearing a path in your lawn is virtually permanent. The spaces between soil particles get "crushed" and that prevents water, fertilizer, or air from getting through easily. The soil becomes like concrete—impenetrable.

The simple test is to take a handful of soil and squish it in the palm of your hand. If it sticks together without falling apart, then it's too wet to work in. Container plants don't use soil, so this rule can't be dragged out to get you off the hook there.

Another reason to avoid working in the yard when it's wet is that fungus or other diseases can be spread more easily in a moist environment. You don't want to help spread problems. (BB)

Fish Gotta Swim, Roots Gotta Breathe

WATER is the source of life but watering is one of the great mysteries of gardening. *Many* people make the mistake of watering too much. That, combined with poor drainage, is the leading cause of death for plants because an excess of water causes a lack of oxygen: without oxygen plants will suffocate.

Before you plant *anything*, ensure that you have proper soil drainage. This is critical for healthy plants (except, of course, for the few that like swampy conditions). In certain climates, such as where I live in the Northwest, frequent rainfall can lead to what is called "wet feet," meaning plants are sitting in water for long periods.

Dig a hole (about 2 feet deep), fill it with water, and wait about an hour. If there is still water in the hole, you don't have good drainage.

One solution for improving soil drainage is combining compost with soil to give it a nice, crumbly texture and increase oxygen flow. Raised garden beds are also great because they allow you to layer good soil right over bad soil. If you're the nonconfrontational type, just choose plants that don't mind getting their feet wet. (JJ)

Plant Like With Like

IN SPRING, all over town I will invariably see all sorts of container plantings—usually outside a retail business—that combine plants that basically don't like one another. No, I'm not talking about something like the Middle East conflict. I'm talking about plants whose differences are so great that they will never be friendly neighbors. Usually, it's a bunch of pansies and something that likes drier conditions—a miniature juniper for example. Sure, it looks really cute, but it won't last.

Plant like with like.

That is, combine plants with growing needs that are similar, such as water and sun. If you plant something that needs lots of water with something that doesn't, neither of them will be very happy for long.

These growing conditions are often referred to as "cultural" requirements and are important bits of information to know about what a plant likes and does not like. It includes water needs, fertilizer needs, sun needs—all the things necessary for it to flourish. So, when you are planning container plantings or beds, keep in mind that good friends make good neighbors. (BB)

All Sun Is Not Created Equal

I AM FROM THE SOUTH, and for several years I also lived in Texas and California. These locales can be hot, hot, *hot*, and, unless you are a lizard, I have learned that finding a shady spot can be a lifesaver. Plants are the same. Although there are many plants whose tags state they prefer "full sun," all sun is not created equal.

Depending on the area of the country in which you live, there's sun and then there's *sun*. This isn't always a simple concept to convey, but sometimes full sun is really too much, even for a plant that loves sun. The same idea applies to part sun and shade. High, filtered shade (such as that cast by a tall tree) may be perfect for a sun-loving plant growing in a really hot climate.

If you live in a hot climate (and you know who you are), then locating a bed in a spot that receives some shade during the day can mean the difference between life and, well, death. You'll just have to experiment to find out. (BB)

Compost Happens

HOW DOES A FOREST feed itself? A forest floor is made of decomposing leaves, branches, and wildlife manure. Decomposing matter feeds new growth and underneath it all is a ton of microbial life that is essential to healthy soil. It's the circle of life that we can (and should!) imitate.

That popular bumper sticker reads a little differently, but the idea is the same: composting *does* happen. I am willing to bet big bucks the reason you may not compost is because you think it will be too time consuming (or take up too much space). *Au contraire*. You will find composting tumblers at your local garden store but these are not necessary. Just use any type of bin or crate (even straw bales arranged in a square, 3 feet by 3 feet) that allows airflow; simply turn your compost every couple weeks with a pitchfork or shovel. Add only biodegradable scraps—green stuff, kitchen scraps, but no meat or fats—to the heap. Unless you live where things don't rot easily (the desert or high Rockies, for example), within a few months you'll have good, healthy, and *free* compost to use. (JJ)

Get To Know Your Dirt

NO ONE CAN BUILD a house without a firm foundation, and the same is true for gardening. One of the most valuable things you can do to become a successful gardener is to get to know your dirt. And what *is* dirt? All soil is composed of different percentages of clay, sand, or silt. The different proportions tell you the kind of dirt you have. So go outside and grab a handful of moist dirt from your lawn. Go on, don't be shy. Give the handful a little squeeze. If the dirt clumps together in your hand, and does not fall apart when you prod it, this is because it contains clay. If the handful clumps together, then falls apart when you poke it, this means you have loamy soil. If the dirt does not clump together at all when you squeeze it, this indicates that your dirt is sandy.

If you find your soil is loamy, that's awesome—because loamy soil is ideal for most plant types. Sand particles are large and hold little water, whereas clay particles are very small and get packed together so that air cannot easily flow through them. However, loamy dirt has a good balance of sand, clay, and silt particles. It absorbs water well and also allows sufficient airflow to reach the roots of the plants.

The best way to improve sandy or clay soil is to incorporate six to eight inches of organic matter, such as compost, to it. This helps fill in the spaces between the sand and clay particles so the dirt can hold in moisture and nutrients. And moisture and nutrients are exactly what your plants need for optimum health.

Turning soil not your thing? You can circumvent a bad soil situation by installing raised beds and filling them with homemade soil. Ingredients for this homemade soil could include compost, peat, coir (a renewable substitute for peat, which is not sustainably harvested), manure, commercial topsoil (use caution; because it is not regulated, all sorts of things are sold as topsoil), and mulch. Check online for other suggestions for creating a good soil; the most important thing is that the soil should be fertile, hold moisture, and drain well.

Once *you* get to know your dirt, introduce plants—and you've got a garden party! (JJ)

Grass *Will* Fight Back

YEARS AGO when I was trying to be serious about riding horses, I had a full-time job, a part-time job, I freelanced, and I rode. I maintained a calendar with specific times noted for each activity. I was busy!

Gardening took a back seat to mowing and sometimes I would literally jog while pushing the mower in order to cut the lawn because I was on such a tight schedule. I was *shocked* to learn that mowing a lawn stimulates growth. The thing about yard work that I truly disliked—mowing—was in fact being encouraged by the number of times I mowed.

In the plant world, pruning stimulates growth, a fact that is usually a good thing. Cutting a shrub back will often reinvigorate it. What I had failed to note is that mowing is the same thing as pruning—and grass will fight back by growing even faster.

If you want to reduce time spent mowing, mow the grass taller (and fewer times), replace the lawn completely, or install one of the slower-growing types of turfgrasses. The lawn *never* sleeps . . . but you'll have time to relax. (BB)

There's More to Roses Than Knock Out®

ALTHOUGH the rose is America's favorite flower, as a plant it can be a diva. Roses need too much food, too much water, too many chemicals, too much time. The Knock Out® series has changed that, but there's more to roses than Knock Out®.

Don't get me wrong—Knock Out® earned its reputation as the poster child for low-care landscape roses. That's why *everyone* has planted them.

But there are types coming from Europe (especially Germany), where many chemicals have been banned, that are bred to be lower-care and mildew- and blackspot-resistant. Although they still need care for fertilizer and water, you'll have lots less maintenance with the new types. By the time this book is out, there will be more; just Google to find the names of some good ones.

And there are lots of antique roses (old strains) that are much less fussy. These are the survivors of the rose world and often have scent, which has been bred out of modern roses. My favorite is 'Perle d'Or', which has wonderfully fragrant blooms. I had one at a house I sold. I still dream about it. (BB)

Get Into Your Plants' Business

PARENTS WERE SUCH A DRAG when you were growing up, weren't they? After one set a ridiculously early curfew, the other played Twenty Questions when you arrived home. Now you can ask yourself, were they control freaks or was that just their way of showing they cared about you?

You should keep track of your garden this closely too. Many plant disasters can be avoided simply by taking a stroll though your garden spaces every day. Take your time and observe everything. You'll be able to catch leaf-eating pests while they are still manageable, before their population grows out of control. It is much easier to nip a small problem in the bud than to try to bring a pest-filled garden back from the brink of disaster.

Be nosy. Get up in your plants' business. Although they may not respond to your Twenty Questions, they'll appreciate it later. (JJ)

No Glove, No Love—
Practice Safe Gardening

DON'T WORRY; this isn't going to be a replay of your middle school sex education class. Gosh, that was embarrassing. But there is an old adage that applies both to Sex Ed and the world of gardening: No glove, no love.

Admittedly, I find myself sometimes tossing off my gloves and digging around in the dirt bare-palmed. The sensation of cool earth in my hands on a hot summer day is alluring. But recently I renewed my commitment to always wear gloves, and here's why. Gloves do more than simply protect your fingernails from dirt. They shield your hands from the drying, cracking, and splitting that occurs with all that digging around.

All those little cuts and scrapes, however seemingly small they may be, are invitations for infection, damage, and scars. It is *dirt*, after all. Additionally, gloves are essential when spreading fertilizers and soil amendments. Even "organic" fertilizers may be chemically synthesized, and therefore may contain ingredients that can burn your skin.

Don't risk it. Remember: No glove, no love. (JJ)

Free Mulch Falls From the Sky Every Year

Many years ago, I was a magazine circulation manager, which means I was a direct-response marketer. I learned there is *nothing* more powerful than the word *free*. Every fall, if you live where there are deciduous trees, there will literally be millions of leaves falling and . . . leaves are free mulch.

It amazes me to see people rake and bag leaves, then leave them at the curb for the city to pick up. Then they will go out and *buy* mulch. You don't have to do that.

There is a difference between compost and mulch, and leaves can be either. For leaf *compost*, the leaves must be *composted* (decomposed) over time. Leaf *mulch* is not left to decompose before using, but it's still a good idea to shred it first. Just pile up the leaves and run over them a few times with a lawnmower. Keep it separate from your compost pile or just use immediately. (If you don't shred the leaves, they can mat down and become a seal over your beds, preventing moisture and oxygen from reaching the soil.)

Free mulch. Falling from the sky. What a country! (BB)

You Don't Have to Have a PhD to Understand pH

SOIL pH TELLS YOU how acidic or alkaline your garden soil is, measured in a range from 0 to 14 (with 7 being neutral). Anything below 7 is acidic and anything above 7 is alkaline. Certain nutrients are only available for plants if the pH is in within the range they need, which is why pH matters.

Most plants like it somewhere in the middle, or slightly acidic. Like everything, there are exceptions: azaleas, rhododendrons, and blueberries like soil that's really acidic; lilacs and clematis like soil that's more alkaline.

How do you know if your soil is acidic or alkaline? You test it. I recommend sending a soil sample to be tested because then experts interpret the results, but you can do this at home using kits. The Extension Service (a free service available wherever there is a land grant university—which is nearly everywhere) will test it for you.

If your soil pH is off-kilter, you can add lime to increase it or sulfur to lower it. It's not easy to change pH, so you may just decide to go with the flow and plant what will grow best in the pH you have. (BB)

Don't Wait Until All Your Leaves Fall

IF YOU LIVE WHERE there are lots of deciduous trees, it's almost inevitable you'll be raking some wet leaves at some point, especially if there is lawn underneath the trees. Unless you're living just right, it *will* rain on those leaves sooner or later.

It's not good to bury lawns under leaves, especially wet ones, because it will smother the grass. So you've got to rake, and often. (However, if you don't have a lawn, or not much of a lawn, I would seriously consider not raking at all. You don't see Mother Nature out there with a rake, do you?)

Wet leaves are heavy (*duh*), but you can make it a little easier by using a tarp (or, if you're über-cheap like I am, an old shower curtain liner) to load leaves on. Drag the tarp to your compost pile or to the spot where you're mowing over the leaves. You can also stuff them into those compostable paper bags as you rake. I found a pair of leaf "claws" that I *love*. They look like giant Frisbies with toothed edges and can pick up a ton of leaves (wet or dry). (BB)

If the Glove Fits, Buy It

I AM WHAT IS POLITELY referred to as frugal, though there are plenty of other words that could be used. For years at the start of every gardening season, I'd buy those cotton gloves that don't fit well and wear through almost immediately. I refused to buy the "good" gloves because I thought the cheap ones were just as good.

They aren't.

Once I bought a pair of well-fitting gloves (goatskin), I realized they are a worthy investment. Since then, I have continued to purchase a few pairs of less expensive gloves at the start of each season, but I always have a good pair as well.

I found I was a better gardener when my gloves fit well: my hands did not get dirty, I could grip tools and plants more easily, and I oddly felt more knowledgeable. There is a great type that's sized to fit a woman's hand, but there are many that are perfectly wonderful including some with "grippy" palms. If you grow roses, those gauntlet-length gloves are really worth the investment to prevent your arms from being ripped to shreds.

So if the glove fits—buy it! (BB)

When in Doubt, Throw It Out

YOU DON'T HAVE TO BE A SCIENTIST with a petri dish to know what happens when biodegradable items are left to their own devices. Remember your old college roommate? The one who left bowls of mac-n-cheese on the floor for weeks at a time? It got crusty, moldy, and attracted an entire colony of ants. Yeah, it was gross then, and it has the potential to be gross in your garden too.

Okay, obviously you're not going to leave half-eaten mac-n-cheese in your garden, but to a hungry swarm of pests, fungus spores, or fast-spreading mold, any veggies and diseased, rotted leaves that fall off the vines are a smorgasbord.

Yes, it's true that decomposition is also your friend, since it is nature's way of creating black gold—compost. However, not only should weak and rotting plants *not* be left in your garden among other healthy and thriving ones, they shouldn't be left in your compost pile either, where diseases can survive and even thrive.

Toss—in the trash—rotting plants, along with any diseased or pest-infested leaves, veggies, or fruits, in order to keep your garden clean and pest free. (JJ)

One Year of Weeds, Seven Years of Seeds

THIS IS ONE OF THOSE GREAT garden sayings that you really should learn. Weeds and native plants—which sometimes *are* weeds—have adapted themselves remarkably well to their environments. Weed seeds can remain viable for seven years (or more!) and remain dormant until the conditions are *just right* for them to germinate. So if weeds are allowed to go to seed, you can count on their seeds springing up, seemingly out of nowhere, for many years to come. Seeds will be brought to the surface by tilling and will sprout as soon as possible. If they're allowed to mature, they will suck your garden dry of moisture and nutrients.

What can you do? Well, you can keep weeds mowed (if they are in an area that can be mowed), or you can snip off the seedheads (deadhead) as soon as possible. You'll have to do this before the seedheads become mature; deadheading just allows them to fall to the ground, unless you collect the seedheads.

In the long run, you will save yourself lots of time and frustration if you deal with the weeds before they can go to seed. Seven years is a long time. (BB)

Give Your Plants a Little Breathing Room

SOME PEOPLE GO CRAZY with a pair of garden shears in order to try to force a giant shrub into submission. Others rather plainly ignore the task of pruning until their junipers are nearly ready to crash through the eaves. You'll be a lot happier if you find a middle ground between these two extremes.

Pruning, sometimes called "thinning," is essential. Not only does it make your trees and other plants look better, it also increases the amount of air flow between them, which is important for eliminating places where pests and diseases can hang out. For some plants, (like roses and blackspot), good air flow is as important to fighting diseases as just about anything else. And limbing up trees can bring much-needed sunlight to the lawn below.

Once I got over my initial hesitation, I learned that it is best to prune no more than one-third of the plant's size in one season. Now I *love* to prune. After a quick snip here and there, my trees look more like they've gotten a snazzy hairdo fresh from the barber than a scraggly mess. (JJ)

A Dwarf Can Still Be a Giant

SEVERAL YEARS AGO, my cousin discovered—the hard way—that a dwarf can still be a giant. It was a Burford holly (ah, those hollies . . .) that had been planted as a foundation plant—and it was up to the eaves. Somehow, when it's little and cute in its tiny container, it kinda looks like a Shitz Shu puppy. But later! Well, it's more like a Great Pyrenees.

In horticultural terms, the word *dwarf* is relative; it just means that a plant is smaller than its parents. In the case of the Burford holly, the nondwarf form can grow up to 15 feet. Sure, the dwarf form is smaller, but that still means it can grow to *six feet tall*. Even if it's not being used as a foundation plant, it can overwhelm the space where you're planning to install it.

If you are looking for a tree or shrub to fit a specific space, there are lots of great options that are naturally smaller. It pays to do a tiny bit of research (this can just mean checking the plant tag) to see what its mature size *could* be—and believe it! (BB)

Just Because It's For Sale Doesn't Mean It Should Be

UNLESS IT'S AN ANNUAL—or a plant you're happy to grow as an annual in your zone—it really pays to ask a few questions before buying a perennial (especially if it's a more expensive tree or shrub).

The big-box stores, in particular, and even some nurseries will sell plants that just don't grow well in your zone. I have learned not to assume that, just because a plant is being offered for sale, it's a good bet. It may be "finicky" or "tricky." Just ask, and if the staff is vague or really can't answer your questions, you'll want to do a little research (which could just be asking your designated garden expert).

Another source, and your taxes pay for it, is the Cooperative Extension Service. It's a nationwide organization within the USDA whose purpose is to help farmers and homeowners with all kinds of plant questions, and pest and disease diagnosis. They offer Master Gardener classes for anyone interested in more education (in exchange for volunteer hours). They love to get calls. (BB)

Test Soil With Your Bare Bottom

THIS IS ONE OF THOSE wise old sayings that happens to be true, and it's so much fun to do.

Frost-free dates refer to two times in the year: the average *last* frost date (in spring) and the average *first* frost date (in fall). Unless you live in a nearly frost-free area, you should wait about two weeks after the average spring frost-free date before planting, to be sure that Jack Frost won't bite you in the behind. Not only can transplants and seedlings get nipped by frost, but most seeds don't like cold soils and they will just sit there, inviting rot.

The next suggestion may sound completely cracked, but the best way to determine if the soil is warm enough to plant seeds of summer flowers and vegetables is to sit on the ground with a naked bottom. If the soil feels cold or cool, wait a few days and try again. If you're squeamish about shocking the neighbors, then just walk across your yard in your bare feet. It's the same idea, although a lot less fun.

I can't wait for spring. Okay, fine, I'll do it at night. (BB)

When Life Gives You Lemons, Make Lemonade

WHEN MY NEIGHBORS BUILT A FENCE to keep their dog from running off, I ended up looking at an ugly fence. What's a girl to do? I created a focal point planting to distract my view of the fence.

If you have an eyesore in your backyard, such as an unsightly heat pump or satellite dish, disguise it with a wooden screen or a beautiful shrub. If you have nosy neighbors lurking around, or a general lack of privacy from the road, find out (quickly) which types of trees and shrubs can create a natural fence. If you have soggy soil, plant plants that like boggy conditions. If the sun beats down on your south-facing wall, abandon your efforts to create a woodland garden and instead learn to love succulents.

When you learn how to take your garden obstacles and turn them into garden triumphs, suddenly they don't seem like such a big deal anymore.

Of course, if Life gives you melons, you know it's dyslexic. (Get it? Lemons, melons . . .). (JJ)

White Roots Are Good Roots (At Least for Plants)

SOMEONE RECENTLY ASKED ME what my natural hair color is, and the truth is, *I don't remember*. It's on my bucket list to try all the colors at some point. So it's a little hard for me to say this, but: white roots are good roots (at least for plants).

This trick is much easier when you're shopping for annuals or perennials but if you can manage it, slip plants out of their containers to check the roots. Roots should be plump, white or light-colored, and generally look healthy. They should not be dark, dry, or stringy.

Like the saying "No hoof, no horse," roots are *critically* important to plant health. There is no substitute—you cannot water enough, fertilize enough, nor nurture enough if a plant is handicapped by a poor root system. (It *is* possible to salvage a plant that is root-bound, which means the roots have grown so long in their container that they are winding round and round. Just whack off some of that excess root growth—it will actually stimulate a plant to grow new roots.)

Take a peek before you buy. It's no fun to pull out dead plants. (BB)

Bigger Isn't Always Better

DO YOU REMEMBER how as a kid, you thought the bigger things were, the better they were? Sure, this rule still applies to chocolate chip cookies and down pillows. But bigger dogs mean bigger piles of you-know-what. A bigger bike means you fall harder when your feet can't touch the ground. And bigger sharks—well, they're just scary no matter what size they are.

Some gardeners recommend buying the biggest plants available. However, this plan is very expensive if you are starting a garden from scratch. The advantage of buying small plants, besides the fact that they are less expensive, is that their root systems will develop in *your* soil, not in the nursery pot. The bigger the plant is at the time you purchase it, the more susceptible it is to transplant shock. Bigger plants are also more likely to be weak and root-bound.

It's better to buy smaller sized plants when you are purchasing ones that will mature quickly (annuals and perennials). With slow-growing trees and shrubs, select larger specimens at a nursery. This is the best way to save money and minimize gaping holes between your plants. (JJ)

Timing Is Everything (When Pruning Flowering Shrubs and Trees)

IT TOOK ME a really long time to realize it, but most shrubs and trees *love* to be pruned. Pruning stimulates stronger and abundant growth, and flowering types have to be pruned to make sure there are plenty of buds for the following season.

The tricky part is knowing *when* to prune. This is not as easy as it sounds. You have to know if it is a spring-bloomer or a summer-bloomer.

Spring-bloomers include forsythia, crabapples, dogwoods, spirea, honeysuckles, redbuds, lilacs, and azaleas. Prune these pretty soon after they finish, because they bloom off old wood, meaning they set buds for the following spring later in the year. If you wait too long to prune, you'll cut off the buds (meaning no flowers the next spring). Summer-bloomers include crape myrtles, butterfly bush, hydrangeas, beautyberry, nandinas, potentilla, and mockorange. Red or yellow twig dogwood is in this group because new growth is more vividly colored. Prune these in late winter or really early spring, because they bloom off new wood.

Late fall isn't a good time to prune either of these types because it might trigger new growth right before winter, and that is not a good thing. (BB)

Only Virgins Should Be Sacrificed to Volcanoes

THERE IS a nationwide epidemic of sacrificing trees to volcanoes—volcano mulching, that is. I don't know exactly when or where it started, but I suspect it's the monkey-see-monkey-do philosophy of mimicking what you think an "expert" is doing.

Homeowners see professional landscapers (and I use those words loosely) building massive mulch towers around trees, ostensibly to protect them, and think it's the right thing to do. I fell for it, and lost a dogwood (which is easy to lose in the best of circumstances) in the process. The bark split open at the mulch line, insects moved in, and I chalked one up to experience.

Trees are not meant to be buried in mulch. By its nature, mulch retains moisture, but that's not always a good thing. If it's not aerated, mulch can actually develop a "skin" that *repels* water. If it's doing its job, mulch can trap too much moisture at the root zone, leading to tree stress. If mulch is piled around the trunk, it is like putting out a welcome mat for insects.

Leave the trees alone, and only sacrifice virgins (if you can find one) to volcanoes. (BB)

Soon Ripe, Soon Rotten

ONE OF THE GREAT THINGS of the slow food movement (eating locally) is a return to growing your own vegetables. Commercial farms grow varieties that are adapted for shipping, and they harvest the vegetables and fruits when they are green because they can literally be in transit for weeks. This is disastrous for flavor.

That's why it's a little shocking to discover that, while it's great to grow your own food, once they ripen—that's it! You really need to eat them (or preserve them in some way) quickly, or they will rot. I recently had a beautiful peach that—overnight— went from almost there to gone. If it has soft skin, like peaches or tomatoes, plan to eat them very soon after picking. Corn on the cob will convert its sugars into starch almost immediately; that's why people joke that you have to have the water boiling as you run out to pick it. If it has a rind, like melons or cucumbers, it will last longer. Another trick is to leave the dirt and tops on veggies until you're ready to eat them. Remember, soon ripe, soon rotten. (BB)

You Can't Grow Grass in a Garage

ONE OF THE FIRST gardeners I listened to was Denny McKeown, the well-known Midwestern radio voice of gardening. One of Denny's many sayings is "you can't grow grass in a garage"—meaning that you have to have sun (and lots of it) to grow turfgrasses.

I'm not so sure *not* being able to grow a lawn is a bad thing, but for the other 95 percent of Americans, having a lush lawn is a thing of beauty. Plus, unless you are happy with bare dirt, you will have to have some sort of groundcover to replace that lawn anyway.

Virtually all turfgrasses need four to six hours of sun per day—any less and the lawn will look like your balding uncle. And grass that's growing under mature trees is especially challenged because most tree roots are within the top 6 to 24 inches of soil. If you really want grass, consider thinning tree limbs, pick a shade-tolerant grass (St. Augustine and fescue are two examples), keep leaves raked, walk on it as little as possible, and don't use herbicides. If you want to give up, there are lots of great groundcovers. (BB)

Super Mario's Got Nothing on Dirt and Worms

KIDS LOVE GETTING DIRTY so much they're natural garden helpers—ones you don't have to pay. And they don't even have to be *your* kids!

Gardening is a great family or community activity. To initially interest kids, don't set any limits to how dirty they get. Or just purchase sets of colorful galoshes that are just right for garden wear. There are lots with funny faces, such as frogs or ladybugs.

Gardening is a great way to introduce children to fascinating insects such as ladybugs and praying mantises. Let them pluck snap peas and cherry tomatoes right off the vine and pop them into their mouths. Kids love dramatic extremes, so plant towering sunflowers right alongside cheerful little morning glories. An easy, fun activity is to plant a sunflower teepee—it's pretty simple, but you can go online for directions. Encourage your kids to touch and feel the different textures of super soft fuzzy lambs' ears, prickly coneflowers, and delicate columbine. Entice them with the lovely fragrances of lemon balm, rosemary, and lavender.

Kids won't even realize you're teaching them about the value of the outdoors, healthy eating, and good ol' fashioned hard work. (JJ)

You Can't Escape
Your Hardscapes

"HARDSCAPE" MEANS all the hard elements in your lawn—driveways, sidewalks, retaining walls, fences, outbuildings, pools, arbors, patios—that you're unlikely to move or change once they're there.

Even if some hardscape component doesn't exist *now*, it's *much* easier to have a general plan in your head before you start gardening so you don't plant a huge balled-and-burlapped maple tree right in the middle of where you'll someday have a pool.

Do you like formal or informal? Lots of lawn or virtually none? Shady or sunny? Write a one- or two-sentence description of your gardening style, what makes you happy, and post it where you can see it. That might have prevented me from buying sections of antique fencing that, to this day, sit in my garage. Or maybe not.

A good landscaper or landscape designer can certainly help you add hardscapes (especially paths and walkways) to an existing mature landscape, but it's trickier to add large hardscapes without having to rip something out. (Frankly, though, you—yes, you!—can design paths and walkways.)

Have a plan so you'll know before you grow. (BB)

Edibles Are the
New Kids on the Block

ANNUALS, perennials, and flowering shrubs aren't the only kids on the block. Many edibles have *spectacular* displays of colorful flowers or leaves, or the fruit itself is gorgeous.

Think of edibles in the same way you would any other plant in your landscape—you don't have to dedicate a large bed just for them. Small space gardens and existing landscaped yards look *great* when interplanted with edibles and ornamentals. People used to designate a bed in a far-off corner of the yard for vegetables but that is so last century!

Edible ornamentals serve a double-duty purpose by indulging both your palate and your color palette. Colorful globes of tomatoes, eggplants, and peppers add interest to any container, bed, or border. Artichoke leaves offer a bold, architectural look. Rhubarb is a nice contrast to airy plants with its broad, glossy, green leaves.

Rather than planting an ornamental groundcover, why not try something edible like lettuces, mesclun mixes, or strawberries? Or plant a fragrant culinary herb garden with thyme, chives, basil, parsley, and cilantro. All of these plants are delicious, and they indulge us twice since we eat with our eyes first. (JJ)

The Drip Line Is a Tree's Dinner Table

I SOMETIMES SEE, often on commercial properties, a huge tree that is being "saved" from the surrounding pavement. While this is commendable, most of these trees are ultimately doomed because too much ground too close to the tree is paved over.

The outermost edge of a tree's canopy of leaves defines what's called its "drip line" and the area underneath it is called the "drip zone." A tree's roots grow to the drip line and stop, and most trees have thousands of feeder rootlets within this area.

This is important because the drip line is like a tree's dinner table. It's where you should feed and water a tree—just inside the edge of a tree's canopy. You don't want to do *anything* that interferes with the drip zone, such as covering it with pavement, surrounding it with a retaining wall, or burying it under too much stuff (such as soil or mulch).

There are things you can use, such as permeable surfaces, if you're paving close to a tree you want to save. The best thing for the tree, though, would be to keep pavement outside the drip line, if possible. (BB)

Deadheading Isn't Just for Rock Concerts

LONG BEFORE the classic band the Grateful Dead developed a cult following, gardeners removed spent flowers, which is called "deadheading." Cutting off shriveled flowers can help plants produce more new blossoms and extend their bloom time. This is because plants are always trying to complete their life cycle by going to seed. When dead flowers are removed, the plants refocus their energy on producing blooms, rather than producing seeds.

You will find that some dead flowers are easier to pinch off than others. Take the threadleaf coreopsis. I love this plant for its little daisylike blooms atop fine, threadlike foliage. However, it is a *nightmare* to pinch off every little flower as they shrivel up, one by one. For this type of plant, it is easier to wait until most of the flowers are spent, and then give the whole plant a nice haircut to about half its size.

In no time at all, threadleaf coreopsis produces more flowers. And it's not the only plant that likes a haircut; dianthus is another example. Be creative in finding the best deadheading techniques for your plants, or ask your local nursery friend for help. (JJ)

In Design, At Least, Opposites *Do* Attract

CONTRAST is a basic element of all design. Fashion, interior, media, architectural, and landscape designers all use contrast, as do photographers and other visual artists. It is essential for creating visual interest.

If you've ever gazed at a garden and thought, *that doesn't look quite right*, it was probably because it lacked contrast. It's tempting for less experienced gardeners to buy plants that are the same size, shape, and color to fill the landscape. One example I immediately think of is the evergreen shrub garden, which simply overpowers yards with too much structure. (And they're even worse if the owner has pruned them into large geometric shapes.) These severe landscapes are in desperate need of some grasses and perennials to soften them up.

To avoid any harsh appearances, experiment with different colors, textures, and shapes. These are the elements that create contrast in any type of design. Mix the fine textures of grasses with broad, glossy leaves; combine concrete or brick hardscapes (meaning patios, walkways, and other flat surfaces) with potted plants; place "chocolate" foliage next to lime green. Use contrast. Mix it up. And your garden will look just right. (JJ)

Repeat, Repeat, Repeat —for Impact

THERE IS A REASON that only a clown would wear a pair of blue-and-yellow striped pants with a green-and-white polka-dot shirt and a bright yellow tie. Too many colors and patterns jumbled together in one small space just look silly (unless you're French, in which case it looks fabulous).

Repetition is one of the basic landscape design elements, and it's something the casual gardener can do easily. Keep in mind it is easier to select plants and landscape materials to suit a theme than it is to make seemingly random, differing plants look good together (like a cottage garden). Leave *that* to professional designers.

Try creating a sense of theme and cohesiveness by repeating a specific type of shrub on different sides of an area, or by repeating a specific plant shape. If you love white flowers, look for different varieties of perennials, annuals, trees, and shrubs that bloom at different times. This way, you can repeat "white" year-round.

The point is not to repeat the same things over and over, but instead to create *repetition with variation* for familiarity and visual interest. (JJ)

More Is More When You're Talking Plants

UNTIL FAIRLY RECENTLY, I was a cheapskate when it came to buying plants. Oh, I'd get a few pansies or narcissus bulbs, for example, but I really didn't get enough to make an impressive show. I'd plant about four or five pansies in a container and call it a day.

But that all changed when I had a few extra pansies I had to do something with. I crammed them into an existing container and was struck by how much *better* the entire thing looked. It works for plants other than pansies too. There's nothing sadder in the world than a skinny line of narcissus or tulips that have that ducks-in-a-row look.

More is more *most* of the time, at least when we're talking plants. There are some plants that benefit from being allowed to demonstrate their form above everything else, though.

The philosophy of "more is more" *really* matters when you're planting skinny plants that need the visual impact of a mass effect to have any kind of presence at all; otherwise, you just won't notice them. (BB)

Feng Shui Your Way to a Gorgeous Garden

THE CHINESE PHILOSOPHY of *feng shui* teaches (among many things; it's a complex topic) that a garden must be free of clutter so your *chi* (creative energy) has an unobstructed path. Free of clutter means picking up fallen tree branches, dried leaves, or decaying plants right away because their presence disrupts the flow of *chi* and lowers the energy level of the area.

A garden should have order, with everything having a specific purpose and place. Each tree, plant, and object is there to balance the five *feng shui* elements: earth, metal (statuary), water (fountains, ponds), wood (trees and shrubs), and fire (red or orange foliage). (*Feng shui* itself translates as "wind/water," so pick up a nice wind chime too.) If something is out of balance—too much or too little—you will feel it.

Part of *feng shui* means living *with* nature, rather than trying to sanitize and conquer it. That means, maybe, leaving even a little part a bit wild.

Even if you think *feng shui* is hooey, its principles are good advice. Personally, I love it. Anything that encourages me to eliminate clutter has got to be a good thing. (BB)

Begin With the End in Mind

THERE'S AN OLD SAYING, "A failure to plan is a plan to fail." One of the most overlooked steps in creating a garden is also the key to success: planning. So many people stop off at the local nursery and pick up a few plants without ever considering *where* these plants will end up, and *how* they can integrate with an existing garden. The thought of narrowing down the choices of a gazillion plants (not to mention garden pots and all the rest) can be paralyzing.

But there's a solution. Ask what you want from your garden space, and how much time you can spend on it, *before* it becomes the "beast that cannot be fed."

If you have children or there are kids running around your neighborhood, avoid expensive, delicate plants that may be ruined by an errant soccer ball. If you love to entertain outdoors, plant large, striking perennials that need little maintenance. Peonies, hostas, and coral bells all make a big impact, and look lovely around a patio or outdoor dining area.

Figure out the purpose of your garden, make a plan, then carry it out so that you enjoy gardening. (JJ)

Simplicity Is the Key to Garden Art

I DO LOVE A LITTLE WHIMSY here and there. But I am really not a fan of concrete bunnies or plastic deer in yards. That just seems a little, well, silly.

Garden ornaments that also function as art, such as benches, plant trellises, stakes, or pieces that mimic the natural shapes and textures of plants, add visual interest, especially when your plants are hibernating in the winter.

One of the keys to adding art to your garden is not to overload your space with too many small things. You want the yard to appear stimulating, interesting, and natural—not like grandma's collection of ceramic teddy bears. Use the basic design element of simplicity: create a theme or select different pieces made of the same materials. I personally love juxtaposing rusted metal elements with my galvanized containers. They differ, but together create a theme and are not cluttered. Consider the style of your home and how you may embellish it with your garden art. And if you are an artist yourself, don't hesitate to feature your own work. That is infinitely more personal and interesting that a concrete bunny. (JJ)

Companion Planting: Carrots *Do* Love Tomatoes

MANY VEGGIES need pollination in order to produce fruit. So it is to your advantage to plant flowers in your vegetable garden in order to attract more bees and other pollinators. You can use this idea of companion planting to protect fragile plants from wind and rain, improve the taste of fruits and vegetables, and even help some plants produce more fruit. But companion planting doesn't stop here.

Carrots Love Tomatoes, a well-known book (from another publisher), is the bible of companion planting, which is based on the idea that certain plants can benefit others when planted next to, or close to one another. Companion planting also benefits certain plants by providing natural pest control, without the need to use chemicals.

One of the most popular companion plants is nasturtium, which attracts caterpillars away from cabbage, broccoli, and cauliflower. African marigolds, which deter aphids with their smell, also attract hover flies to *eat* the aphids.

Companions aren't always flowers; there are countless other combinations you can find by Googling "companion plants." Because even in the world of flora, friends gotta have each others' backs. (JJ)

The Color Wheel
of Fortune

ONE OF THE AREAS in which many—dare I
say, most—people feel uncomfortable is regarding
garden design. It's true for me. But if you borrow
some ideas from interior designers, especially using
the color wheel, many decisions about color are
simplified. Understanding or even knowledge of
the color wheel is so lacking in garden centers and
nurseries that it's a little shocking. It's often up to
you to know about it and know how to use color in
the garden.

The easiest color scheme is monochromatic; that
is, all one color. It could be a white garden (beautiful
at night), or a green garden (easier and prettier
than it sounds). The hardest thing to pull off is the
polychromatic garden (lots of mixed colors). It's like
the Longfellow poem: "When she was good, she was
very good indeed, but when she was bad she was
horrid." It can be done, and that delightful hodge-
podge English cottage garden look is full of mixed
colors, but that can be a goal more than your first
attempt at garden design. Interior designers also
often recommend adding a touch of white or yellow
to perk up a room. It can be just a little, but it adds a
"pop!" of color that's really refreshing.

The color wheel shows primary, secondary, tertiary, and neutral colors. Primaries are reds, yellows, and blues. Secondary colors are greens, violets (purples), and oranges. Tertiary colors are blends of primary and secondary colors. Neutrals are white, grays, and silvers. (Note: Neutral colors come from mixing equal amounts of complementary colors. Violet and yellow made a neutral beige, green and red make a different brown, and so forth.) The idea is to find a color style you like (warm colors, cool colors) and add complementary and contrasting colors until you have something that works. You can get ideas from public landscaping: most suburban neighborhoods, for example, have hideous landscaping at their entrances, but some are fantastic. There's no shame in copying what the good ones are doing. (If *you* like it, it's good.)

But flowers bloom at different times of the year. So if you like the idea of yellow in your garden, you may want to have yellow daffodils and black-eyed Susans in the same bed because they will bloom at different times. And fall! Well, that's more limited but you can use mums or another container plant for color then.

Just start with your favorite season to get a little design confidence and branch out from there. Rest assured the garden will wait for you. (BB)

Gardens Are Like Women— More Beautiful With Curves

MAYBE IT'S LEFT OVER from our childhoods, but there's a sense of safety that comes from staying within the lines. And that could be why most garden spaces are rigidly geometric, made up of various sizes of squares and rectangles with sharp corners. Interestingly, you will rarely find geometric shapes occurring in nature. Instead, curves are *everywhere*: curling leaves, snaking branches, billowing clouds, and meandering forest trails. There's a reason Marilyn Monroe, who had curves from here to there and everywhere in between, is still known as the world's sexiest pinup. Curves are welcoming, create a naturalistic feeling, and invite a lingering air of free movement. This doesn't apply just to Marilyn's hips; it applies to your landscape. One dramatic curve can keep a space from feeling cold.

Straight lines have their purpose, as they may be used to direct attention to a focal point. Curves, in contrast, will create a more organic feeling. You may not want your lawn's dimensions to be 36-24-36, but long, swooping curves are definitely more casual and natural-looking than all straight lines and boxes. (JJ)

Teed Off Plants
Are Happy Plants

BECAUSE THEIR FOLIAGE will sometimes disappear (bulbs, for example), it's not always easy to remember where perennials are in your yard. You can invest in some really cool plant markers; I feel very botanic garden when I use them. But there's a really great and inexpensive solution. Golf tees are (often) small, virtually impossible to see unless you know they're there, and they're cheap!

Golf tees are great to mark spots where bulbs are planted so you don't dig them up in fall, mow over them in spring, or plant over them because you *think* you know what's there. If you're a control freak, you can color-code the tees to indicate the type of bulbs underneath. (If that's the case, I urge you to get help.) If you like to vegetable garden, and plant less than full rows, you can use a golf tee to mark the spot where you switch from one veggie to another.

Another more natural way to mark the location of other plants is to use daylilies or some grassy foliaged plant. (BB)

Plant Iris (and Azaleas and Rhododendrons) Like Ducks Sitting on the Water

IT'S VERY TEMPTING to plant everything the same way. You dig a hole (crossed fingers that it's larger than the container or root-ball you're planting) so that the plant is sitting at the same depth it was. That's true for most plants, but not all.

Iris, azaleas, and rhododendrons are all planted sitting a little "high," like ducks sitting on the water. That is, partly in the soil, partly out of the soil. One year, I was given many (and I mean *many*) iris divisions. I was very busy at the time, so I literally dropped them on top of the earth in one of my beds. Not only did they live, but they lived large! (Iris really should be planted in about 1 to 2 inches of soil, but mine did fine sitting right on top; they eventually rooted themselves.) Peonies are another plant that doesn't like being planted deeply; just plant them 1 to 2 inches down and don't smother them with mulch.

It was my first experience that some plants don't like to be planted deeply. Read the plant tag or check online to make sure. You might save yourself some digging! (BB)

How to Get Two Plants for the Price of One

NURSERIES DON'T REALLY LIKE you to know this, but there are lots of plants that can be divided *before* you even plant them. That way, you can get two plants for the price of one! I wouldn't do this with annuals but perennials should be able to catch up and fill in the bed.

Some of the easier plants to divide are daylilies, hostas, sedums, and ornamental grasses. They spread in clumps, so they eventually will need to be divided anyway at some point.

Pick ones that are really healthy—they should look healthy and be large enough (probably a gallon size) to cut apart. When you're ready to plant, carefully take them out of the pot and use a knife (literally) or scissors to cut them in half. I have a pair of garden shears that I love for this purpose. Each section should have some roots and stems.

Don't worry if you're cutting some roots; as long as you don't mangle things they should be okay. Then just plant as you normally would—but you'll have twice as many! Who doesn't love a bargain? (BB)

Trees & Shrubs Are Like Teenagers; Annuals & Perennials Are Like Children

IF YOU TRY to balance gardening with the rest of your life, bear in mind that trees and shrubs are a bit like teenagers, or litterbox-trained cats. They can pretty much exist on their own, with some occasional pruning and maintenance. You can leave for a few days (or longer) and they will be just fine.

Annuals and perennials, on the other hand, are like children; they simply need more attention. It would be difficult (and, frankly, illegal for anyone who's thinking of this) to leave children alone for any length of time; they are fairly high-maintenance creatures. Even if annuals or perennials are planted in well-mulched beds, they will need watering, fertilizing, and weeding at some point, usually several times a season.

If at least one of your garden goals includes time management, consider whether you have time for high-maintenance plantings. Oh, and here's the thing about containers—they probably need the most attention of all, because they dry out so quickly. Not only are plants in containers affected by sun, but wind is extremely drying. Sometimes, in summer, I water the container plants morning *and* evening. (BB)

Out of Sight Is Out of Mind

If you are a new gardener, you may feel compelled to sow in every available sunny spot, sill, and corner. But this is not always the best option. I went through three artichoke plants before I understood the reason they kept dying on me. Each artichoke withered away in the hot summer sun before bearing fruit because I kept planting them in a spot with other mature perennials and mature grasses—a location that literally was taking care of itself. The artichokes were out of sight and mind, and I *always* forgot to water them.

If you dare to venture into the world of high-maintenance plants (such as artichokes), then do yourself a favor and plant them in a convenient place for you to consistently monitor and water them. If there's an area of your yard where you would like to have some plants, but don't visit very often, buy inexpensive and dependable plants that are able to thrive with little help from you.

The "plant 'em and forget 'em" plants will be different for different parts of the country, but I guarantee you there will be at least one of every plant type. (JJ)

No Yard? No Problem

IF YOU ARE ONE of the several million or so people have a small backyard, or none at all—no problem! You can still be a gardener, even if you don't have a lot of space. One word: containers.

Got a patio or a windowsill? Then you have room for some plants. Just make sure that your spot will receive about four hours of sunlight a day. Dig colorful, fragrant flowers? Hibiscus and scented geraniums do well in containers in a sunny spot. Multitasking herbs such as oregano, rosemary, and chives offer ornamentation, fragrance, and flavor. Really, pretty much any herb will grow well in a patio pot or on a windowsill, as long as you trim it back to keep it nice and compact.

Even if you live in a high-rise apartment with shaded windowsills, all hope is not lost. In shady spots, try houseplants such as sanseveria (mother-in-law's tongue) and philodendron. In all cases, make sure to water your plants when the soil becomes dry and crumbly, as container plants tend to dry out more rapidly than plants in the ground.

Now, take *that*, naysayers. Who says you can't garden without a yard? (JJ)

Spiky, Roundy, Frilly, Floppy: The Container Garden Formula

THE RULE OF "spiky, roundy, frilly, floppy" is fairly well known in the gardening world, but I felt I had discovered El Dorado when I heard it described the first time. It's a "formula" for designing a container planting. You pick at least one of each of these shapes (forms), in the colors you like (complementary or not), and have at it!

Once I knew this rule, I felt a burden had been lifted from my shoulders, because the area in which I feel the least amount of gardening confidence is garden design. But everyone can pick out forms! And guess what? It works perfectly. The spiky part is a tall plant; the roundy component is a plant that is, well, round; the frilly element is a plant that has interesting leaf edges; and the floppy part is a trailing plant. Find plants in colors you like, which have the same requirements for sun and water, and *voilà*!

Another way of thinking of container design is to combine the "thrillers, fillers, and spillers." Either way, it's container plant magic! (BB)

Shake and Bake to Reuse Potting Soil

POTTING SOIL IS the medium that's used in containers. It's not really soil; that would be too heavy and compact too much. It's soil-*like*, a sterile mix of things like bark (composted), peat moss, sand, perlite, and sometimes fertilizers or moisture-retaining pellets. There are special blends for different types of plants, such as orchids, African violets, and cacti, which have different combinations of the basic ingredients (cacti mix has more sand, for example).

Americans spend about $500 million annually on potting soil. You *can* make your own mix (though I'd rather slit my wrists), but I rarely completely replace mine. Just dump the potting soil from containers into a wheelbarrow and pick out the leftover roots, leaves, and any naughty bits. Then let it sit in the sun for a few days to bake (I do this in early spring). I'll mix in some fresh potting soil (sometimes with the fertilizer added in) and fluff it all up. The fluffing part is the key—it needs to be airy. Then scoop it back into your containers. Every few years, I do replace potting soil completely and throw the old stuff in my compost pile. (BB)

Containers Will Bloom Where They Are Planted

IF YOU GARDEN ON A BALCONY or front porch, then really your only choice is container gardening. But even if you have a decent-sized patch of dirt to work with, containers are an excellent way to enhance your landscape design. I have several different containers tucked into all my garden beds. They allow me to plant small shrubs and trees near existing ones without disrupting root systems and to overwinter plants such as perennials and ornamental grasses.

One situation in which container gardening served me well was when I needed a practical way to disguise my neighbor's ugly fence. I invested in a *huge* ceramic container, and planted a red-leaved Japanese maple, then skirted the edges with Japanese forest grass and blood grass. Not only does it look great, but I see what *I* want to see—not that ugly fence.

Other practical places to put containers are in areas that do not have good drainage and spaces that you would like to draw attention to. To create a focal point, choose colored containers that contrast with what you have planted. Then tie that color into other areas of the garden to create a cohesive appearance. (JJ)

Grow Up—Use the Space You Have

GROW UP—vertical gardening, that is. Vertical gardening is ideal for the small lawns of urban areas, balcony gardening, or if you are looking for ways to use the space you have. As a general rule, anything that can be grown in a hanging basket, like strawberries, can grow up.

The most important key to remember is that you must support plants. Just as a seven-story building will not stand without the proper joists and beams, neither will your cucumber plants stand without a fence, arbor, stake, or trellis. Think of your supports in terms of your available space.

Practice the same garden rules as you would in a ground-bound garden. Plant diseases and some pests can still reach plants even if you're several stories up. Some insects are not vertical crawlers, yet both slugs and snails found their way to the top of my living wall, and stopped along the way to nibble my lettuces. (JJ)

Bambi and Thumper Are Only Cute in Disney Movies

IN ANIMATED DISNEY MOVIES, those cuddly rabbits and long-lashed deer *look so cute*! You'd never think in real life you would want to kill them. Both of these voracious critters can do *lots* of damage in your garden, and there's not much you can do about it.

To control rabbits, you can use rabbit fencing, which has a wider mesh than chicken wire, around valuable plants. Or you can put it up as a true fence; just make sure you bury it several inches into the ground so rabbits can't dig under it.

Deer are harder to control. You can install a deer fence (which has to be several feet high) but that's really expensive and not practical. There are special deer repellents, but you have to spray them repeatedly (especially after it rains). I've heard that human hair will scare them off (it scares me; that stuff's spooky). And strong-smelling soap hung from branches is also supposed to work.

You can also plant "deer-proof" plants that deer don't *usually* like, such as iris, daffodils, alliums (onions), most herbs, butterfly bush, cotoneaster, viburnums, and magnolias. But deer love hostas, tulips, lilies, and yews. Good luck. (BB)

Your Garden Is Around All Year

FLOWERS ARE THE FIRST PLANTS that lure most beginning gardeners—all those colors and shapes! I love flowers myself, but it didn't take me long to figure out that perennial flowers only look pretty for one season, then wither away after they do their thing to build up storage reserves for the next year. But my garden will be there for another three seasons before the perennial flowers return!

To avoid a complete state of garden hibernation in this downtime, mix multiseason foliage into your garden beds. When your gorgeous pink and blue asters are crumpled and brown, the bright foliage of euphorbias, sedums, and coral bells can take the stage. Plant dark green and purple chameleon plants that are winter hardy and will look nice even when the salvias next to them stand like skeletons. For a garden that looks good all year, don't confine foliage plants to a separate bed.

Garden sculptures and evergreen shrubs also create interest in your garden during winter (or whenever the "off" season is). Planting evergreens or spiky ornamental grasses will bring color and form to the scene even when your pretties are not in bloom. Think about adding bushes that set berries in winter, such as hawthorn and chokeberry, or deciduous bushes like red or yellow twig dogwoods, whose bare branches can be appreciated in winter. Once they're in place, there's little maintenance.

And even some flowers look really fabulous when they are covered with seedheads, especially when those seedheads are topped with little fluffy mounds of snow, as happens where I live. Of course, before you allow your flowers to go to seed you should note that some, like cleome or hollyhock, could add a lot more weeding to your agenda the following spring, when the seeds they dropped begin to sprout everywhere.

I let my coneflowers, yarrow, black-eyed Susans, Siberian irises, and *Sedum* 'Autumn Joy' produce seedheads, and leave them in my garden all winter. These all add a cool element of texture and shape while also providing the birds with food. The seedheads' rich brown colors become more dramatic when backed by tall decorative grasses like miscanthus.

Surprisingly, dead plants can create a very interesting structural element in your garden. As one of my favorite landscape designers says, "Dying, in an interesting way, is just as important as living." (JJ)

Me Talk Latin One Day

HAVE YOU READ the David Sedaris book *Me Talk Pretty One Day*? It's about the difficulties humans have communicating, and he uses his hilarious adventures mangling the language in France to illustrate his points. I know exactly how he feels. When I attempt to speak botanical Latin (or, frankly, any kind of Latin), it's not a pretty sight.

But it is useful to learn some basic Latin to understand the concept of botanic nomenclature (the scientific method of naming plants), which is based on genus and species. Once you know the relationships among and between plants, you will also know something about their characteristics. For example, the genus name *Hydrangea* is derived from the Greek word for water, so it's not surprising that a hydrangea *loves* water. The species name *sanguinea* means "blood" or "blood red," indicating that some part of the plant will be red.

There sometimes is a cultivar name (an abbreviation for "CULTIvated VARiety") enclosed within single quotes that follow the species name. A cultivar's traits will be consistent, which is pretty handy to know. Plus, you'll sound really, really smart when you can reel off some botanical Latin. (BB)

If You Can Throw It,
You Can Grow It

I SOMETIMES PROCRASTINATE buying annuals until all the healthy, good plants are sold— not just from the nurseries, but also from the big-box stores. Now, that's pretty late in the season. One year I was desperate for some color, so I literally threw marigold seed (left from the previous year) onto the surface of my pots. I didn't even cover them with potting soil.

And they *grew*! Not only did this not require a green thumb, it didn't require any thumb at all. Marigolds, zinnias, sunflowers, cosmos, celosia, globe amaranth, morning glory, and coleus are all annuals I've easily grown from seed (though not always as late as the marigold story).

The point is there is *something* that you can grow. It may not be a "showy" plant but nothing says it has to be. There are lots of "little" plants that are virtually foolproof, can easily be grown from seed, and can be grown for summer color even if you start a bit late in the year. Just read the seed packages to see how easy they are to grow or ask a neighbor for ideas. You might even get some free seeds! (BB)

If Your Tree Falls Into Your Neighbor's Yard, Will There Be a Sound?

TRICK QUESTION! Yes, there will be a sound. Or several.

I found this out when an enormous pine tree in my backyard just fell over one day after a particularly long spell of rainy weather. I had known that the tree was leaning, and had even thought about having it removed. Sadly, I did nothing.

Once the tree fell, I "generously"—or so I thought—offered to split the cost of removal with my neighbors. Even though the law considers the responsibility of removal to be the burden of the homeowner upon whose property the tree falls, the truth is that creating bad feeling with your neighbor over a fallen tree isn't worth what you'd pay to take care of the situation.

By the time it was over, we no longer spoke to each other. They removed the *half* of the tree on *their* property but refused to allow access to me to remove the remainder (the tree removal company would have had to cross their property to access it).

If I had the chance to do it over, I would just pay for all of the removal to save the relationship. Be neighborly whenever possible. (BB)

Fifty Ways to Leave Your Zucchini

IT IS A COMMON TEMPTATION for beginning edible gardeners to plant too many of the same thing all at once, resulting in "garden glut." Just about everyone has ended up with more of something than he or she knows what to do with. Even if you are *crazy* about squash, it's hard to find enough ways to serve a harvest of zucchini that is piled up to your armpits. Sure, you can pass some along to your neighbors. But even your best friends won't be thrilled by handfuls of foot-long zucchinis.

Focus on planting only what you and your family can eat during harvest season, along with a little for canning or freezing if you're into that. Here are some tips on how to estimate how much to plant: a 100-square-foot garden—that's two 4-by-12-foot beds—is enough to feed a family of four during a growing season. A typical raised bed may have three to five tomato plants, two hills each of cucumbers and summer squash, or three poles of runner beans. The key is to plant in blocks (square-foot gardening) or wide rows—single rows waste space. (JJ)

Herbs Hate Wet Feet— True or False? Yes

ONE YEAR WHEN I was a child, I received a cactus as a Christmas gift (yes, I thought that was odd too). I didn't know *anything* about plants, so I faithfully watered it until it literally fell over as I delivered the *coup d'etat*. I had killed it with kindness. You could do this to other plants too.

It's tempting to treat herbs just like vegetables because they are edibles, but herbs like things a little rough. Those that are referred to as "Mediterranean"—parsley, sage, rosemary, thyme, tarragon, oregano, and lavender, for example—evolved in sunny, windy conditions in really rocky, alkaline soil. That is, in rock! The more you duplicate those conditions, the happier they will be.

But while some herbs *hate* getting their feet wet, that's not always true for every one. Mints *love* water, as does watercress (surprise!) and basil. Read the plant tags to make sure. If you are growing a water-lover, you can investigate those cool little water globes that you stick into your container or in the ground to help them stay watered. A dried-up basil plant is a terrible thing to waste. (BB)

"I Did" Beats "I Will" Every Time

I USED TO work in advertising (and I have the scars to prove it), and I learned to recognize a good advertising slogan when I saw one. They are rarer than you might think. Nike's "Just Do It" slogan —so simple, so complete—is nearly perfect. Not only is it a motivator for sports, it can be considered a life mantra.

In gardening, having an "I Did" philosophy is invaluable. If you want a water feature, you should have one. You don't have to install a fountain to rival the Bellagio; you can start small with a wall fountain. Just do it.

If you have a condo with only a small patio and want to garden—you can. You will be amazed at how much you can do with very little space, especially if you garden up! Just do it.

If you want professional help designing your landscape, start small with one section or bed. I hired a landscape designer to create a plan for the area between my front sidewalk and the house itself. The design was affordable, as was the installation, but the effect is priceless! Just do it. (BB)

You Can't Download Experience

IT'S TRUE: Experience counts. That's why the best-paying jobs will always require a candidate with experience, often years of it.

Although the purpose of this book is to give you the "CliffsNotes" rules of gardening that we learned the hard way, to be a gardener, you have to garden. Over time, you will learn all kinds of tricks, especially as it relates to your personality, your climate, and your garden space. If you aren't really interested in gardening, you'll still learn all kinds of shortcuts to maintain your yard the way you like it.

But even though you can't download experience (at least, not yet), it doesn't mean you can't learn some valuable things from the Internet, magazines, and books. There is everything from YouTube videos of planting bulbs to organic gardening methods to garden design tips on the Internet. There are all kinds of specialty magazines, many of which feature great how-to design tips or urban gardening. And books, especially those oriented to specific states or regions, can really cut to the chase when it comes to valuable tips.

Beware, though, of getting information from sources other than local ones, mainly from England. It seems odd in a way that our bookstores are stuffed with books that were originally published in England. But just think about it: the English have magnificent gardens and lots of garden books are published to satisfy the English gardener. But often those books are just reissued for the American market. It doesn't help that the British books are often beautifully illustrated with lots of color photographs of lovely plants and great gardens. But their climate and range of plants (not to mention diseases, pests, types of soil, and range of sunlight) is so *totally* outside that of the United States that a bunch of the information inside just doesn't apply to us.

Check the copyright page; if you can't tell the country of origin, read through some of the book. The spelling of certain words might give it away. Or read the author's bio; does it sound like the writer is English? If yes, pass on by.

If you *are* ready to learn more about gardening, then check out the page at the back of this book. Books written for a regional audience means you don't have to waste time unlearning something that doesn't apply to your area. (BB)

There's No Substitute for a Quality Tool

WHEN YOU'RE STARTING OUT, you'll only need basic tools for weeding, digging, and pruning. Depending on the size of your garden, the minimum you will need is a shovel, rake, hoe, hand trowel, bypass pruners, and a means of watering. Don't automatically reach for the cheapest brand, since these are quite likely to quickly break or rust—you'll end up spending twice as much as you intended by having to replace them. Look for tools made of steel as opposed to cheap metals like aluminum; the best have handles made from wood, but you'll need to oil them to prevent splitting. Purchase the best tools your budget will allow.

Later, if you decide you need to add to your toolbox, there are plenty of additional tools and gadgets from which to choose. For example, a cultivator to aerate or break up soil, a pruning saw or long-handled pruners, and a wheelbarrow or cart can be very handy. And don't forget gloves and a sun hat!

Protect your investment. Clean your tools off after using them, and make sure they are dry before you store them in order to prevent rust. A little TLC goes a long way. (JJ)

My Garden Rules

Glossary

Alkaline soil: soil with a pH greater than 7.0. It lacks acidity, often because it has limestone in it.

All-purpose fertilizer: powdered, liquid, or granular fertilizer with a balanced proportion of the three key nutrients—nitrogen (N), phosphorus (P), and potassium (K). It is suitable for maintenance nutrition for most plants.

Annual: a plant that lives its entire life in one season. It is genetically determined to germinate, grow, flower, set seed, and die the same year.

Bare root: describes plants that have been packaged without any soil around their roots. (Often young shrubs and trees purchased through the mail arrive with their exposed roots covered with moist peat or sphagnum moss, sawdust, or similar material, and wrapped in plastic.)

Beneficial insects: insects or their larvae that prey on pest organisms and their eggs. Examples are ladybugs, parasitic wasps, praying mantids, soldier bugs, predatory nematodes, spiders, and ants.

Canopy: the overhead branching area of a tree, usually including foliage.

Cold hardiness: the ability of a perennial plant to survive the winter cold in a particular area.

Compost: organic matter that has undergone progressive decomposition by microbial and macrobial activity until it is reduced to a spongy, fluffy texture. Compost improves the soil's ability to hold air and water and to drain well.

Cultivar: a CULTIvated VARiety. It is a naturally occurring form of a plant that has been identified as special or superior and is purposely selected for propagation and production.

Deadhead: a pruning technique that removes faded flower heads from plants to improve their appearances, abort seed production, and stimulate further flowering.

Deciduous plants: trees and shrubs that lose their leaves in fall.

Desiccation: drying out of foliage tissues, usually due to drought or wind.

Division: the practice of splitting apart perennial plants to create several smaller-rooted segments. The practice is useful for controlling the plant's size and for acquiring more plants; it is also essential to the health and continued flowering of certain ones.

Dormancy: the period, usually the winter, when perennial plants temporarily cease active growth and rest. Dormant is the verb form, as used in this sentence: Some plants, like spring-blooming bulbs, go dormant in the summer.

Established: the point at which a newly planted tree, shrub, or flower begins to produce new growth, either foliage or stems. This is an indication that the roots have recovered from transplant shock and have begun to grow and spread.

Evergreen: perennial plants that do not lose their foliage annually with the onset of winter. Needled or broadleaf foliage will persist and continues to function on a plant through one or more winters, aging and dropping unobtrusively in cycles of three or four years or more.

Floret: a tiny flower, usually one of many forming a cluster that comprises a single blossom.

Germinate: to sprout. Germination is a fertile seed's first stage of development.

Hardscape: the permanent, structural, nonplant part of a landscape, such as walls, sheds, pools, patios, arbors, and walkways.

Herbaceous: plants having fleshy or soft stems that die back with frost.

Hybrid: a plant that is the result of intentional or natural cross-pollination between two or more plants of the same species or genus.

Low water demand: describes plants that tolerate dry soil for varying periods of time. Typically, they have succulent, hairy, or silvery-gray foliage and tuberous roots or taproots.

Mulch: a layer of material over bare soil to protect it from erosion and compaction by rain, and to discourage weeds. It may be inorganic (gravel, fabric) or organic (wood chips, bark, pine needles, chopped leaves).

Naturalize: (a) to plant seeds, bulbs, or plants in a random, informal pattern as they would appear in their natural habitats; (b) to adapt to and spread throughout adopted habitats (a tendency of some nonnative plants).

Organic matter: any material or debris that is derived from plants. It is carbon-based material capable of undergoing decomposition.

Peat moss: organic matter from peat sedges (United States) or sphagnum mosses (Canada), often used to improve soil texture. The acidity of sphagnum peat moss makes it ideal for boosting or maintaining soil acidity while also improving its drainage.

Perennial: a flowering plant that lives two or more seasons. Many die back with frost, but their roots survive and generate new shoots in spring.

pH: a measurement of the relative acidity (low pH) or alkalinity (high pH) of soil or water based on a scale of 0 to 14, 7 being neutral. Individual plants require soil to be within a certain range so that nutrients can dissolve in moisture and be available to them.

Pinch: to remove tender stems and/or leaves by pressing them between thumb and forefinger. This pruning technique encourages branching, compactness, and flowering in plants, or it removes aphids clustered at growing tips.

Rootbound (or **potbound**): the condition of a plant that has been confined in a container too long, its roots having been forced to wrap around themselves and even swell out of the container. Successful transplanting or repotting requires untangling and trimming away of some of the matted roots.

Self-seeding: the tendency of some plants to sow their seeds freely around the yard to create many seedlings the following season.

Semievergreen: tending to be evergreen in a mild climate but deciduous in a rigorous one.

Slow-acting fertilizer: fertilizer that is water insoluble and therefore releases its nutrients gradually as a function of soil temperature, moisture, and related microbial activity. Typically granular, it may be organic or synthetic.

Succulent growth: the sometimes undesirable production of fleshy, water-storing leaves or stems that results from overfertilization.

Sucker: a new-growing shoot. Underground plant roots produce suckers to form new stems and spread by means of these suckering roots to form large plantings, or colonies. Some plants produce root suckers or branch suckers as a result of pruning or wounding.

Variegated: having various colors or color patterns. The term usually refers to plant foliage that is streaked, edged, blotched, or mottled with a contrasting color—often green with yellow, cream, or white.

You Talk Latin One Day

Sometimes people feel uncomfortable with botanical names. The words are unfamiliar and sometimes long and hard to pronounce. Why don't garden books just use common names instead?

There are several reasons that books and catalogs give both botanical and common names. Mostly, it's to avoid confusion. Common names for a plant vary from place to place. You and a neighbor, who grew up in a different state, may call the same plant by different common names. One plant may also have collected a number of different common names, adding to the confusion.

So every plant has a botanical name—usually Latin, occasionally Latinized Greek—that belongs to it and it alone. If you are looking for a particular plant at a local garden center or from a mail-order nursery, you'll find it by the botanical name. If you need to ask advice about a plant from the Extension Service or another expert, they can readily identify your plant by its botanical name.

Another reason for using botanical names is that, once you look at them carefully, you'll pick up clues to what the plant is like. *Alba* means white, for instance. *Japonica* tells you that the plant originated in Japan, while *canadensis* tells you the plant was originally found in Canada. *Citrina* indicates lemony yellow. In leaf shapes, *lancifolia* is lance-leafed, *crispula* may be curled, *undulata* may be wavy, and *serrata* indicates serrated leaves. *Variegata* obviously indicates variegation (more than one color on a leaf). *Sempervirens* is evergreen. As part of a species name, *micro* means very small, *grandis* is large, and *gracilis* is slender.

The first word in a plant's botanical name (which is always capitalized and italicized) is the genus name; think of it as a family name. It's a group of plants that are closely related—*Hosta*, for instance. The second name (which begins with a lowercase letter and is also italicized) is the species, which identifies a distinct type of individual plant, such as *Hosta fortunei*. The third name (which may be more than one word) is the variety or cultivar name. In botanical terms, there are differences between varieties and cultivars but in popular gardening language, they're used interchangeably. Cultivar stands for **cult**ivated **var**iety. It's a plant that was selected for its desirable qualities from a larger group of plants. The cultivar name is usually enclosed in single quotation marks. For example, *Hosta fortunei* 'Albopicta' further identifies the hosta as a particular cultivar.

What Did You Say?

But how do you pronounce all those tongue-twisting words? That's why the following pronunciation guide is provided—to give you the confidence to ask for a plant and talk about it by its botanical name. Consider it a guide only. Different experts have varying ways of pronouncing some of these names. In most of the U.S., for example, we say "stokesia" as stow-KEY-zee-uh. In England, and among some professionals in this country, it's pronounced STOKES-ee-uh, after the man for whom the plant was named. So, you'll hear it both ways.

Not to worry. You already know how to pronounce many more botanical names than you think. You're not so sure? Well, what about these—impatiens, petunia, salvia, begonia, zinnia, canna, crocus, dahlia, iris, zoysia, phlox, vinca, sedum, camellia, forsythia, hibiscus, nandina, rhododendron, viburnum, magnolia, hydrangea, and wisteria? See, you already have a head start on pronouncing botanical names.

Pronunciations

Ageratum, *Ageratum houstonianum* (ah-jer-AY-tum hous-tone-ee-AN-um)
American holly, *Ilex opaca* (I-lex o-PAY-kuh)
Anemone, *Anemone* × *hybrida* (uh-NEM-o-nee high-BRED-duh)
Artemisia, *Artemisia* (ar-te-MEEZ-ee-uh)
Arum, *Arum italicum* (AIR-um i-TAL-i-cum)
Aucuba, *Aucuba japonica* (ah-Q-bah juh-PON-ik-uh)

Bald cypress, *Taxodium distichum* (tax-O-dee-um DIS-ti-kum)
Baptisia, *Baptisia* species and hybrids (bap-TIZ-ee-uh)
Beautyberry, *Callicarpa* species and hybrids (kal-i-CAR-puh)
Bermuda grass, *Cynodon dactylon* (SIGH-no-don DACK-tih-lon)
Black-eyed Susan, *Rudbeckia* species and hybrids (rood-BEK-ee-uh)
Bleeding heart, *Dicentra spectabilis* (die-SEN-tra spek-TAH-bil-iss)
Bluebeard, *Caryopteris incana* (kar-ee-OP-ter-iss in-can-a)
Boltonia, *Boltonia asteroides* (bowl-TONE-ee-uh as-ter-OY-deez)
Boxwood, *Buxus* species and hybrids (BUCKS-us)
Buckeye, *Aesculus* species and hybrids (ESS-ku-lus)
Bugleweed, *Ajuga reptans* (a-JOO-guh REP-tans)

Burning bush, *Euonymus alatus* (u-ON-e-mus a-LAY-tus)
Butterfly bush, *Buddleia davidii* species and hybrids
   (BUD-lee-uh day-VID-ee-eye)
Butterfly weed, *Asclepias tuberosa* (as-KLEE-pee-us too-buh-RO-suh)

Caladium, *Caladium bicolor* (kuh-LAY-dee-um BYE-cull-er)
Camellia, *Camellia* species and hybrids (ka-MEAL-yuh ja-PON-ick-uh)
Canadian hemlock, *Tsuga canadensis* (TSOO-gah can-uh-DEN-sis)
Candytuft, *Iberis sempervirens* (eye-BEER-is sem-per-VIE-renz)
Canna, *Canna* species and hybrids (KAN-nuh)
Cardinal flower, *Lobelia cardinalis* (lo-BEE-lee-a kar-di-NAH-lis)
Carex, *Carex* species and hybrids (CARE-ex)
Carolina allspice, *Calycanthus floridus* (kal-i-KAN-thus FLOOR-i-dus)
Carolina jessamine, *Gelsemium sempervirens*
   (jell-SEE-mee-um sem-per-VIE-renz)
Carolina silverbell, *Halesia tetraptera* (huh-LEE-zi-uh tee-TRAP-ter-uh)
Cattail, *Typha* species (TIE-fuh)
Celosia, *Celosia argentea plumosa*
   (seh-LOW-see-uh r-JEN-tee-uh plew-MO-suh)
Chaste tree, *Vitex agnus-castus* (VIE-tex AG-nus-KAS-tus)
Chrysanthemum, *Dendranthema × grandiflorum*
   (Den-DRAN-thuh-muh gran-dih-FLOOR-um)
Clematis, *Clematis* species and hybrids (KLEM-a-tis)
Cleome, *Cleome hasslerana* (klee-OH-mee hass-ler-AH-nuh)
Climbing hydrangea, *Hydrangea anomala* (hy-DRAN-gee uh-NOM-uh-luh)
Coleus, *Solenostemon scutellarioides*
   (sol-eh-no-STEH-mon scoo-tuh-LOID-eez)
Columbine, *Aquilegia* species and hybrids (ack-wi-LEE-gee-uh)
Coreopsis, *Coreopsis grandiflora* (ko-ree-OP-sis gran-di-FLOOR-uh)
Cosmos, *Cosmos bipinnatus* (KOZ-mose bi-pin-NAY-tus)
Crape myrtle, *Lagerstroemia* species and hybrids (lay-gear-STRO-me-uh)
Creeping juniper, *Juniperus* species and hybrids (jew-NIP-er-us)
Creeping phlox, *Phlox* species and hybrids (flocks)
Creeping thyme, *Thymus praecox* (TIME-us PRE-cox)
Crocus, *Crocus* species and hybrids (CROW-kus)
Crossvine, *Bignonia capreolata* (big-KNOWN-ee-uh cap-ree-o-LA-tuh)

Daffodil, *Narcissus* (nar-SIS-sus)
Dahlia, *Dahlia* species and hybrids (DAL-ya)
Daylily, *Hemerocallis* hybrids (hem-er-oh-KAL-iss)
Deciduous azalea, *Rhododendron* species and hybrids (row-doe-DEN-dron)
Deciduous holly, *Ilex* species and hybrids (EYE-lex)
Dianthus, *Dianthus* species and hybrids (die-AN-thus)
Dogwood, *Cornus* species and hybrids (KOR-nus)

English ivy, *Hedera helix* (HED-er-uh HE-licks)
Epimedium, *Epimedium* species and hybrids (ep-uh-MEE-dee-um)
Evergreen azalea, *Rhododendron* hybrids (row-doe-DEN-dron)
Evergreen holly, *Ilex* species and hybrids (EYE-lex)

False cypress, *Chamaecyparis* species and hybrids (kam-uh-SIP-a-ris)
Feather reed grass, *Calamagrostis acutiflora*
  (kal-a-ma-GROS-tiss ah-ku-ti-FLOOR-uh)
Five-leaf akebia, *Akebia quinata* (a-KEE-bi-a kwi-NAY-tuh)
Flowering cherry, *Prunus* species and hybrids (PROO-nus)
Flowering quince, *Chaenomeles* species and hybrids (key-NOM-uh-leez)
Foamflower, *Tiarella* species and hybrids (tee-a-REL-a)
Fothergilla, *Fothergilla* species (father-GILL-uh)
Fountain grass, *Pennisetum* species and hybrids (pen-ni-SEE-tum)
Forsythia, *Forsythia* species and hybrids (for-SITH-ee-uh)
Foxglove, *Digitalis* species and hybrids (di-ji-TAL-liss)
Fringe tree, *Chionanthus virginicus* (ki-o-NAN-thus ver-GIN-i-kus)

Gaillardia, *Gaillardia grandiflora* (gay-LAR-dee-uh gran-di-FLOOR-uh)
Geranium, *Pelargonium* species and hybrids (pel-ar-GO-nee-um)
Ginkgo, *Ginkgo biloba* (GING-ko bi-LOW-buh)
Globe amaranth, *Gomphrena globosa* (gom-FREE-nah glow-BOE-sah)
Golden rain tree, *Koelreuteria paniculata*
  (kol-roo-TEER-ee-uh pan-ick-you-LAY-tuh)
Gold flame honeysuckle, *Lonicera × heckrottii* (lon-ISS-er-a hek-ROT-ti-eye)
Goldenrod, *Solidago* species and hybrids (sol-ih-DAY-go)
Grape hyacinth, *Muscari* species and hybrids (mus-CARE-ee)

Hardy begonia, *Begonia grandis* (beh-GOAN-ee-a GRAN-dis)
Hakone grass, *Hakonechloa macra* (hah-koh-neh-KLOH-uh MACK-rah)
Heuchera, *Heuchera* species and hybrids (HEW-ker-uh)
Hosta, *Hosta* species and hybrids (HOSS-tuh)
Hyacinth bean, *Dolichos lablab* (DOL-li-kos LAB-lab)
Hydrangea, *Hydrangea* species and hybrids (high-DRAN-gee-uh)

Impatiens, *Impatiens walleriana* (im-PAY-shens wall-er-ee-AY-nuh)
Iris, *Iris* species and hybrids (EYE-ris)

Japanese blood grass, *Imperata cylindrica* 'Rubra'
  (im-per-AH-tuh si-LIN-drih-kuh)
Japanese cryptomeria, *Cryptomeria japonica*
  (krip-toe-MEER-ree-uh ja-PON-i-cuh)
Japanese maple, *Acer palmatum* (ACE-er pall-MAY-tum)
Japanese zelkova, *Zelkova serrata* (zel-KO-vuh ser-RAY-tuh)
Joe-Pye weed, *Eupatorium purpureum* (you-pa-TOE-ree-um pur-pu-REE-um)

Kentucky bluegrass, *Poa pratensis* (POE-uh pruh-TEN-sis)
Kerria, *Kerria japonica* (KER-ee-uh ja-PON-ick-uh)
Kolomitka vine, *Actinidia* species (ak-ti-NID-ee-uh)

Lacebark elm, *Ulmus parvifolia* (UL-mus par-vi-FO-lee-uh)
Lenten rose, *Helleborus orientalis* (hell-e-BORE-us or-ih-en-TAL-iss)
Leucothoe, *Leucothoe* species and hybrids (loo-KOTH-oh-ee)
Lily, *Lilium* species hybrids (LIL-ee-um)
Liriope, *Liriope* species and hybrids (li-RIE-oh-pee)
Loropetalum, *Loropetalum chinense* (lor-row-PET-a-lum chi-NIN-see)
Lotus, *Nelumbo* species (nee-LUM-bo)
Lycoris, *Lycoris* species (lie-KORR-is)

Madagasgar periwinkle, *Catharanthus roseus* (cath-ah-RAN-thus ROE-see-us)
Mandevilla, *Mandevilla* × *amoena* (man-dee-VIL-luh a-MEE-na)
Marigold, *Tagetes* species and hybrids (TAH-jeh-teez)
Melampodium, *Melampodium paludosum*
  (mel-um-PO-dee-um pal-you-DOE-sum)
Miscanthus, *Miscanthus sinensis* (mis-KAN-thus si-NEN-sis)
Mondo grass, *Ophiopogon japonicus* (oh-fee-oh-PO-gon ja-PON-ih-cus)
Moonflower, *Ipomoea alba* (ip-po-MEE-uh AL-ba)
Moss rose, *Portulaca grandiflora* (por-tyew-LACK-uh gran-dih-FLOOR-uh)

Nandina, *Nandina domestica* (nan-DEE-nuh do-MES-ti-cuh)
New Guinea impatiens, *Impatiens hawkeri* (im-PAY-shens HAWK-er-eye)

Oak, *Quercus* species and hybrids (KWER-kus)
Ornamental cabbage, *Brassica oleracea* (BRASS-ih-kah ohl-er-AY-cee-uh)
Ornamental pear, *Pyrus calleryana* (PIE-rus kal-er-ee-A-nuh)
Ornamental pepper, *Capsicum annuum* (CAP-sih-come AN-you-um)

Pachysandra, *Pachysandra* species and hybrids (pack-ih-SAN-dra)
Pampas grass, *Cortaderia selloana* (kor-ta-DEE-ree-a sel-low-AN-nuh)
Pansy, *Viola* × *wittrockiana* (vy-OH-lah wit-rock-ee-AY-nuh)
Paperbark maple, *Acer griseum* (ACE-er GRIS-ee-um)
Passionflower, *Passiflora* species (pas-si-FLOOR-uh)
Pentas, *Pentas lanceolata* (PEN-tas lan-cee-oh-LAY-tah)
Peony, *Paeonia lactiflora* (pee-OH-nee-uh lac-ti-FLOOR-uh)
Petunia, *Petunia* × *hybrida* (peh-TUNE-ee-uh Hy-BRED-uh)
Phlox, *Phlox* species and hybrids (flocks)
Pickerel weed, *Pontederia cordata* (Pon-the-DEE-ree-uh kor-DAY-tuh)
Pulmonaria, *Pulmonaria* species and hybrids (pull-mom-AIR-ee-uh)
Purple coneflower, *Echinacea purpurea* (ek-ih-NAY-see-uh pur-pu-RE-uh)

Redbud, *Cercis canadensis* (SER-sis kan-a-DEN-sis)
Red maple, *Acer rubrum* (ACE-er RU-brum)
Red salvia, *Salvia* species and hybrids (SAL-vee-ah)
Red valerian, *Centranthus ruber* (ken-TRAN-thus ROO-ber)
Redvein enkianthus, *Enkianthus campanulatus*
   (en-key-AN-thus kam-pan-u-LAY-tus)
Rhododendron, *Rhododendron* species and hybrids (row-doe-DEN-dron)
River birch, *Betula nigra* (BET-u-la NIGH-gra)
Rose, *Rosa* species and hybrids (RO-zuh)

Salvia, *Salvia* species and hybrids (SAL-vee-uh)
Saucer magnolia, *Magnolia soulangiana* (mag-NO-lee-uh sue-lan-gee-A-nuh)
Scaveola, *Scaveola* (skuh-VOH-lah)
Sedum 'Autumn Joy', *Sedum × telephium* 'Autumn Joy'
   (SEE-dum the-LEF-ee-um)
Serviceberry, *Amelanchier* species and hybrids (am-e-LANG-kee-er)
Shasta daisy, *Leucanthemum × superbum* (loo-KAN-thuh-mum × soo-PER-bum)
Smoke tree, *Cotinus coggygria* (ko-TIE-nus ko-GIG-ree-uh)
Snapdragon, *Antirrhinum majus* (an-tir-RHY-num MAY-jus)
Snow-on-the-mountain, *Euphorbia marginata* (you-FORB-ee-uh mar-gin-AY-tuh)
Sourwood, *Oxydendrum arboreum* (ox-ee-DEN-drum ar-BO-re-um)
Southern magnolia, *Magnolia grandiflora* (mag-NO-lee-uh gran-di-FLOOR-uh)
Spanish bluebell, *Hyacinthoides hispanica*
   (hy-ah-sin-THOY-deez his-PAN-ih-kuh)
Spirea, *Spiraea* species and hybrids (spy-REE-uh)
Spotted dead nettle, *Lamium maculatum* (LAY-mee-um mac-u-LA-tum)
Sundrops, *Oenothera fruticosa* (ee-NOTH-er-a fru-ti-CO-suh)
Summersweet, *Clethra alnifolia* (KLETH-ruh al-ni-FO-lee-uh)
Sunflower, *Helianthus annuus* (hee-lee-AN-thuss AN-yew-us)
Sweet alyssum, *Lobularia maritima* (lob-you-LAIR-ee-uh mah-RIT-ih-mah)
Sweet box, *Sarcococca hookeriana humilis*
   (sar-koh-KOH-uh hook-er-ih-A-nuh hum-uh-lis)
Sweet gum, *Liquidambar styraciflua* (lick-wid-AM-bar sti-rah-see-FLOW-uh)
Switch grass, *Panicum virgatum* (PAN-i-kum ver-GAY-tum)

Tall fescue, *Festuca arundinacea* (fes-TOO-ka a-RUN-de-nay-see-uh)
Trumpet honeysuckle, *Lonicera sempervirens* (lon-ISS-er-a sem-per-VI-renz)
Tulip, *Tulipa* species and hybrids (TOO-lih-pa)
Tulip poplar, *Liriodendron tulipifera* (leer-ee-oh-DEN-dron two-lih-PIF-er-uh)

Viburnum, *Viburnum* species and hybrids (vie-BURR-num)
Vinca, *Vinca minor* (VING-ka MY-ner)
Virginia sweetspire, *Itea virginica* (eye-TEE-uh ver-GIN-i-kuh)

Waterlily, *Nymphaea* species (nim-FAY-a)
Wax begonia, *Begonia* × *semperflorens-cultorum*
   (beh-GOAN-ee-uh sem-per-FLOR-ens cull-TORE-um)
Wild ginger, *Asarum* species and hybrids (a-SAIR-um)
Wisteria, *Wisteria* species and hybrids (wis-TEE-ree-uh)
Witch hazel, *Hamamelis* species and hybrids (ham-uh-MEL-is)

Yarrow, *Achillea* species and hybrids (a-kil-LEE-uh)
Yellowwood, *Cladrastis kentukea* (klad-RAST-iss ken-TUK-ee-uh)

Zinnia, *Zinnia* species and hybrids (ZIN-nee-uh)
Zoysia, *Zoysia* species (ZOY-ziah)

Many thanks to author Judy Lowe, who allowed us to use this glossary and Latin pronunciation guide from her book *Tennessee & Kentucky Gardener's Guide* (Cool Springs Press 2001). These pronunciations are listed in common name order rather than Latin name order because that's how you are likely to know them. But, it's possible that a plant can have a different common name in different parts of the country.

Meet Jayme Jenkins

JAYME JENKINS is a former sales rep who left the corporate world to start her own online store specializing in modern home  and garden décor, aHa! Modern Living. Jayme co-hosts Nest in Style, a podcast featuring fellow garden experts and interesting garden-related topics. Jayme stays connected by hosting two blogs, the podcast, and numerous Social Media profiles, but loves to unplug from the Internet world through various activities like mountain biking, hiking, do-it-yourself projects, cooking, and entertaining. Jayme knows firsthand the challenges of being an entrepreneur and balancing a full-time career with her busy lifestyle. Jayme strongly believes in the connection among gardening, design, and environmental responsibility, and encourages others to live this way. You can follow Jayme at her blog (aHa! Home & Garden), via her podcast (Nest in Style), on Twitter (aHa! Modern Living, Nest in Style, Jayme Jenkins, Garden Rules Book), and on Facebook (Jayme Jenkins, aHa! Modern Living, Nest in Style). Jayme Jenkins lives in Eugene, Oregon.

Meet Billie Brownell

BILLIE BROWNELL spent many years in the corporate worlds of marketing, advertising, and publishing from Scripps-Howard to *PC World* magazine, to the largest ad agency in the Southeast, to Cool Springs Press. Billie tries to balance being an editor, writer, aspiring author of children's books, and a gardener with her passion for riding horses. She knows how to cut to the chase to fit it all in, although this partly means

rising at 5 a.m. In addition to taking care of her horse Keillor (named for Garrison Keillor), Billie volunteers at a therapeutic riding facility and serves as the self-nominated cruise director for all who will allow it. You can keep up with Billie on Facebook, Twitter, and through her blogs at Garden Writers Today and The Fence Post for Cool Springs Press. Billie Brownell lives in Nashville, Tennessee.

Plants Can't Read—
But *You* Can!

All gardening is local; it's *your* yard, after all. Cool Springs Press is the leading publisher of local gardening books—written just for where you live. We have hundreds of titles full of reliable and practical advice for people just like you. Visit our website at **www.coolspringspress.com**.

COOL SPRINGS PRESS
Growing Successful Gardeners™